Happy

Sara

With Love on your

9th Birthday.

from Ronnie
        & Maria

x a a

The Young Rider's Handbook

The Young Rider's Handbook

Angela Sayer

Hamlyn
London · New York · Sydney · Toronto

Acknowledgements

Illustrations by Gerald Whitcomb.

Photographs
All by Animal Graphics/Solitaire, Crawley, with the exception: of Animal Graphics, Crawley 23 (left), 30, 96, 107, 113, 126, 161; E. D. Lacey Collection, Leatherhead 178; Ardea Photographics, London – John Daniels 120; Radio Times Hulton Picture Library 53 (inset); Animal Photography, London – Sally Anne Thompson 62, 143 (right), 207, 216; Spectrum Colour Library, London 198/9; ZEFA, London – Damm 6/7.

The author would like to thank the children and ponies of Homewoodgate Farm, East Chiltington, Sussex, for their help in the production of the photographs for this book.

Published 1980 by
The Hamlyn Publishing Group Limited
London · New York · Sydney · Toronto
Astronaut House, Feltham, Middlesex, England

ISBN 0 600 39540 5

Printed in Italy

Contents

Introduction

Millions of young people all round the world enjoy pony riding. This is hardly surprising as it is such a delightful pursuit – what nicer way is there to spend a sunny Saturday afternoon than clopping down a leafy lane, cantering across a heath or going on a mounted picnic ride with friends?

However, there's a lot more to riding than just getting up and going! With this enjoyment must come responsibility and there is, of course, the *care* of the pony to consider, too. Although you will never know *everything* about the subject – it is far too broad and complex – it is important to have a firm, basic understanding of why the pony behaves the way he does, why it is essential to be firm but kind and considerate at all times, to learn that there is more to pony-care than just keeping him clean and well fed. And this is when *The Young Rider's Handbook* becomes essential reading. Crammed full with charts, diagrams and photographs, and a glossary and a list of useful addresses at the back, it looks in depth at every aspect of pony care – as well as riding.

It shows what to look out for when buying a pony, gives full details of all the pedigree ponies and tells you everything you need to know about tack. There is a comprehensive section on first aid, accompanied by

useful diagrams; it explains how to care for both a pony at grass and a stabled pony; there's a chapter on

riding and jumping, and one on all the different ways you can enjoy your pony. Finally, there are lots of vital facts and tips about competitive riding, both inside and outside the ring.

The Young Rider's Handbook is an invaluable guide for anyone who is either just a keen rider or who owns their own pony and wants to enjoy him to the full.

Happy riding!

Choosing a Pony

Unless you are an expert, you should take along a knowledgeable friend when choosing a pony. Buying the right mount takes time and patience and it is important that the pony is suitable for your purpose. It would be futile to buy a 'blood' animal with an excitable nature and a thin coat if your pony is to be used only for weekend hacking and must live out all winter. It would be equally foolish to select a sturdy crossbred cob-type if your aspirations happen to lean towards winning dressage competitions.

Acquiring your own pony is like making a very good friend and is not to be compared with buying a bicycle! You will want to keep him for a long time and so a little extra thought and time taken in choosing the perfect pony is more than well spent.

The best way to buy a pony is from friends or neighbours who have an outgrown family favourite. In this way, you will have a ready knowledge of his faults and virtues from the beginning. The worst way to buy a pony is from a market or

It is well worth taking a little extra time and trouble to find the pony which will suit all your requirements. This will ensure that he is not outgrown for some years.

horse-fair, unless you are able to trace the animal's background before the sale.

In between these two extremes there are the horse magazines and periodicals which run classified advertisements of horses and ponies for sale, and the reputable dealers' yards.

A family pony need not be a beauty and can be of any colour, but he must be of a convenient size and should have a kind temperament and no bad habits. Most beginners feel safest on small ponies, but these are soon outgrown and a pony of 13 to 14 hands (a hand is 10.1 centimetres or 4 inches) is generally suitable for all members of the family to ride and enjoy. When only one pony is kept in a riding family, it is important that he is strong enough to take the adults out for gentle hacking, and quiet and docile enough to carry even the youngest member of the family in complete safety.

HORSE	used generally to describe the whole species, or when differentiating between a horse and pony, to describe an animal over 14·2 hands high. Correctly used means a stallion, or entire male.
STALLION	an entire male horse over 4 years old.
MARE	a female horse or pony over the age of 4.
PONY	a small 'horse' up to 14·2 hands high.
GELDING	a male which has been gelded, i.e. has its reproductive organs removed; this is sometimes referred to as having been 'cut'.
COLT	a young stallion up to the age of 4, described by age, i.e. a yearling colt, two-year-old colt.
FILLY	a young mare up to the age of 4, described by age as above.
FOAL	a horse or pony under one year of age, described by sex as either a colt foal or a filly foal.

Mare or Gelding?

When you find the pony that best suits your needs it will not generally matter too much whether it is a mare or a gelding. A mare is often thought to show more intelligence, and can be very affectionate. Then again, everyone who has owned horses and ponies of both sexes has known very affectionate and intelligent geldings! Mares come into breeding season

at regular intervals, and this can be a disadvantage if they are inclined to be temperamental during those periods. For this reason, some people prefer geldings for general riding purposes.

Stallions are never used as general riding ponies, although there are ridden classes at most shows for stallions and, very occasionally, pony stallions are shown under saddle by quite young riders. The colts are usually gelded from the age of six months. This ensures that, if well handled and properly reared as youngsters, they grow up to be amenable, easily trained riding ponies.

Conformation

Although looks are not of prime importance in a general purpose pony, poor conformation can adversely affect the way the animal moves and so makes him a very uncomfortable ride. Some conformation faults can even make the pony too dangerous to ride.

A pony with a large heavy head is always unbalanced, for he is unwilling to carry it in the correct position. A short thick neck has the same effect, and the rider often feels that he is supporting the head and neck by means of the reins.

A pony with a ewe neck (a neck which, when viewed in profile, curves inwards from the head to the body along its upper line) may carry his head too high and can be alarming to ride. When jumping, the incorrect head carriage causes the animal to jump with a hollow back.

Riding-ponies should have good withers, which prevent the saddle from slipping forward, and good sloping shoulders. Straight shoulders cause jerky up-and-down paces: perfectly acceptable in a driving pony, but most uncomfortable in one used for riding. The space

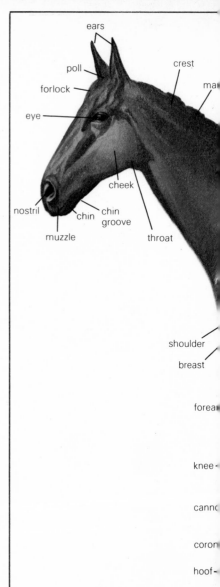

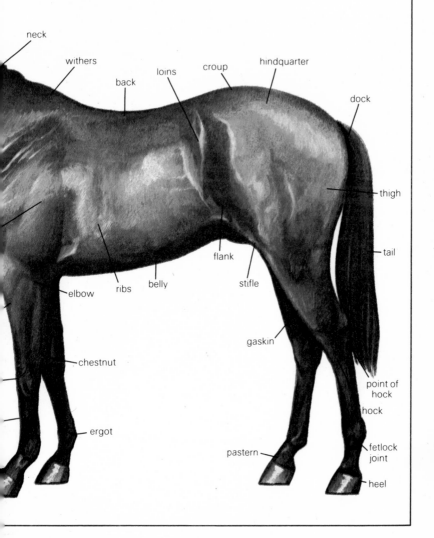

Points of a Horse

neck
withers
back
loins
croup
hindquarter
dock
thigh
tail
elbow
ribs
belly
flank
stifle
gaskin
chestnut
point of hock
hock
ergot
pastern
fetlock joint
heel

When buying a pony, look for a good sloping shoulder.

between the front legs is known as heart-room, and should be well developed. Some badly reared ponies have virtually no heart-room, and their front legs are so close together that their knees and fetlocks brush at all paces. Such ponies are quite unsafe for riding purposes and should be avoided.

The forelegs must be straight when viewed from the front of the pony, and the elbows should stand out so that you can place your fist snugly in the cavities they form with the body. A pony with pinched-in elbows will be clumsy and inclined to stumble. The knees should be sharply defined, with a flat, chiselled effect. The leg above the knee is

called the forearm, and must be strong and muscular. Below the knee is the short, strong cannon bone, joined to the pastern by the fetlock joint. The pastern acts as a shock absorption system, and should be relatively long and sloping.

The pastern joins the hoof at the coronet with a fringe of hair. This hair should not touch the ground at the heel of the pony as this could indicate trouble in the sole of the foot. The hooves should be smooth and hard and look well cared for.

The length of the back varies considerably in ponies. Those with very short backs and deep rib cages always look well rounded and are easy to keep in good condition. They

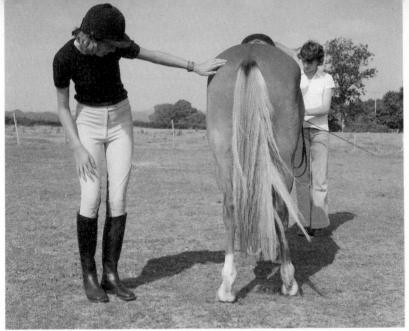

Viewed from the rear, the hocks should be straight, with well-chiselled bone structure.

are comfortable to ride and jump well, with heads in the correct position and rounded backs. Those with very long backs often have a long gap between the last ribs and the hip-joints. This causes the belly to curve up and in, and even when really well fed, such ponies can appear to be in poor condition.

Good quarters and a well-set on tail add to a pony's apperance as well as giving good paces, and there should be no slackness or weakness in the loins. When viewed from behind, the hind legs should be straight. If the hocks incline towards each other, this is a condition known as being cow-hocked: a weakness, but not too important in

a family pony. When viewed from the side, the thigh and gaskin should be well-muscled, the hock joint well formed and chiselled, like the knee. Inside each of the legs will be found small horny growths known as chestnuts. Smaller, similar growths, called ergots, are present on each fetlock. These serve no useful purpose and are thought to be the last vestiges of the prehistoric horses' extra toes.

Examining the pony

Having tracked down a suitable pony for sale, the next step is to go to inspect and try him. It is better to take your first look at the potential purchase while he is turned out in his field. In this way you can determine whether or not the pony is friendly and easy to catch. See if he will let you attach the rope to his head collar and lead him quietly through the gate. If he is already caught up and stabled, talk to him quietly and notice his reactions. An aggressive or distrustful pony may show the whites of his eyes, lay his ears back and tuck in his tail. The gentle, friendly pony will look round with pricked ears and an alert, friendly expression, and may give a little whicker of greeting.

After patting the pony you should look him over for conformation faults, then pick up his feet one by one in turn, to examine them carefully and also to note the pony's reaction. (Instructions about how to pick up a pony's feet are on pages 131/132.) The pony should be shod. beware of buying an unshod pony, for although the reason could be

The pony's temperament may be estimated from his eyes, which should preferably look kind and intelligent. Ponies with white-rimmed eyes may be bad-tempered.

The pony should be shod and have sound, well-formed feet. The hooves should be smooth with no cracks or ridges which might suggest previous attacks of laminitis.

quite legitimate, in that he has been turned out to grass for some time, it *could* mean that he is difficult, or perhaps impossible to shoe. Blacksmiths are in great demand, and do not take kindly to shoeing awkward ponies.

Take your hand along the loins and over the quarters to the tail, hold this firmly then walk slowly and deliberately round the hindquarters, as closely as possible to the other side, watching the pony's behaviour. If his ears go back, or he tentatively lifts a hind leg, he could be difficult.

After this preliminary examination, the pony should be led out and trotted in a straight line away from you, so that you can assess his soundness and action. He should then be turned and trotted directly

towards you. The action should be straight and the hind feet should follow in the tracks of the forefeet. Some perfectly presentable ponies flick their feet inwards as they move, an action known as plaiting. This is not important unless there are signs of cuts or bruises caused by this action on the opposing legs. The opposite action, when the feet are flicked outwards, is known as dishing, and rarely causes problems although both conditions would count as faulty conformation in the show ring.

After trotting up, the pony should be stood up for your inspection with his forelegs close together and one hind leg slightly in advance of the other; he should stand quietly alert while you walk around to look at him from all angles.

When trying out a new pony he is first led out in hand. He should move easily and willingly with an even, free stride.

Back in the loosebox, the pony should now be saddled and bridled while you watch. You should note how he accepts the bit into his mouth, as well as his reaction to the tightening of the girth. Mares generally lay their ears back and even pretend to nip when the girth is tightened. This is merely a mild protest against the tickle. Geldings occasionally object to girthing too, but only when a lifted hind foot, accompanied by tail swishing, is apparent need the pony be avoided completely.

When the pony is properly tacked-up he can be mounted and tried out.

If you are a competent rider you can do this yourself, otherwise the experienced friend should try the pony while you observe.

Trying the pony

First lead the pony out, noting whether or not he follows easily and willingly. Change over to the other side and lead him in the other hand. Note if he leads equally well on either side, if he turns easily, trots on, and stops when asked. When you are quite satisfied that he does what he is asked, put the reins back over his head, take the stirrups down and check the girth before mounting.

Mount smoothly and carefully and note whether or not the pony stands quietly. Does he try to nip you as you mount? Does he try to move off before you have settled in the saddle? Ask him to stand for a moment before moving on, and fiddle with the stirrup leathers or girth to test his reactions. The perfect pony will stand, patiently waiting to be given his next instructions. Young ponies may fidget and fret, but in a good-humoured way. Difficult ponies prance and dance, making it almost impossible to climb aboard. These ponies should be avoided, for you may have to re-mount after a tumble, or in heavy traffic, or in the exciting atmosphere of the hunting field. If a pony will not stand quietly while being mounted in his own yard, he will be impossible at other times.

Notice how quietly the pony stands for mounting; he shouldn't attempt to move forward or sideways, or show any tendency to nip.

When you are comfortably settled in the saddle you can check the pony's conformation from a rider's point of view. There should be plenty of pony in front of you. The head should be carried well, the ears pricked and alert, neck slightly flexed at the crest. The alert pony will also play with the bit while he waits for you to ask him to move off. Look behind you – you should see broad, round quarters. You should

The pony's temperament may be tested, for example by suddenly clapping loudly.

and the cadence of the movement. The trot should be easy, with long free strides. Bring him back to the walk and stop, noting how many strides it takes. Is he easy to stop? Does he resist the bit? Does he swerve, or stop in the desired straight line? If he swerves, is it his fault or could your leg aids be better?

When you are confident that you understand each other and that you can stop him easily, walk and trot again before collecting him and going into the canter. Try to get him going smoothly, on the correct leading leg and not too fast, then change reins by crossing the area diagonally at the trot before cantering off again on the opposing circle. Note whether or not the pony keeps calm at the faster paces, or if he shows any signs of hotting up and getting over-excited. When pulling up, try to do this smoothly and, when stationary, stand the pony up well, correctly balanced on all four legs.

Now is the time to try elementary movements such as reining back, and turns on the forehand and haunches. You may also be able to try opening and closing a gate without dismounting. A few low jumps should be taken, and it is the pony's attitude to jumping rather than his aptitude that is being tested. A perfect pony will approach the jumps calmly and willingly. Unschooled but eager ponies rush at them happily. Lazy ponies jump grudgingly with ears laid back,

also be able to see the tail if it is set and carried well. Drop your hands to the withers, relaxing the reins and make a loud and sudden noise. A quiet pony will stand quite still, others could end up in the next field. Another good test is to wave a whip around to make sure that the pony is not whip-shy. The reins should be gently tightened in turn and the pony's head will move slightly in response unless he is hard-mouthed on either side.

Give the aids (see page 163) to move on. The pony should move forward freely and evenly. Note if he needs kicking, and what happens to his head carriage as he goes forward. When he is moving well at the walk, change direction two or three times before asking him to trot.

Again note the head carriage

18

short, thick neck

ewe neck

good neck

A pony with a short thick neck may find it impossible to carry his head correctly, while one with a ewe neck is likely to jump in an alarming, hollow-backed manner.

they may trail their hindlegs, or even stop.

If there is a horse-box or trailer available, it is a good idea to see if the pony will load and unload without any trouble.

Finally, the most important test of all is to check that the pony is traffic-proof, for even the most experienced of riders is at risk when taking a traffic-shy pony out on the road. Test the pony first on a reasonably quiet road, then have him exposed to some large vehicle if possible. He may tense up a little as it passes but should not swerve or shy.

Whether or not the pony seems to suit all your requirements, you should make the trying session reasonably brief, and you should certainly not gallop about unnecessarily, or try any large jumps. If he

does seem to fit the bill, you should arrange for your own, or an independent veterinary surgeon to carry out the prescribed examination for soundness.

The warranty

When the veterinary surgeon is asked by a buyer to examine a pony for soundness, his responsibilities are to the person paying the fee. His professional opinion on the pony can be given orally or in writing, but obviously the latter, in the form of an official certificate, is the most acceptable. The vet will carry out a most intensive physical examination of the pony, usually watching the animal for any signs of vices such as windsucking or crib-biting, before starting to look him over more closely.

The first check is usually in the mouth, for it is by the dentition that the pony's age can be most accurately determined. Then the pony will be checked from the tip of his nose to the very soles of his feet. His heart and lungs will be tested, first at rest, then after he's had some short sharp exercise.

Then his exact height will be measured. To do this, the pony is stood up on level ground with all four feet in alignment. A special measuring stick is used to determine the distance from the ground to the highest point of the pony's withers, and the measurement is given in hands.

Height

A pony is generally thought of as being up to the height of 14.2 hands. Anything over this is a horse, although the fine animals of the Arabian bloodlines are always known as Arabian horses, never ponies, even if they only attain 14 hands in height. Conversely, the horses used in the game of polo are usually about 15.1 hands high, but they are always referred to as polo ponies. The diminutive Shetland ponies stand alone, as they are measured in centimetres or inches instead of in hands. In show classes, limited by height, 12.7 millimetres or half an inch either way is allowed for the difference in wear of the shoes. Horses and ponies can be officially measured by specially appointed veterinary surgeons from the beginning of February until the end of September each year. Annual certificates are written for ponies 4 to 5 years of age and at 6 years when a pony has ceased to grow, a life certificate can be issued.

The age of a pony is generally determined by a detailed inspection of its teeth.

To issue a health certificate, the vet must first thoroughly examine the pony.

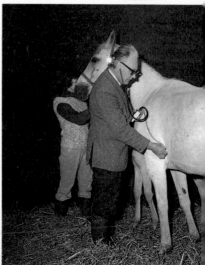

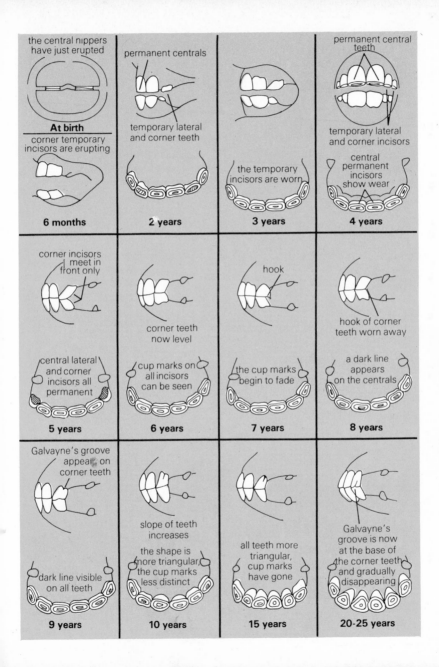

At birth / the central nippers have just erupted

6 months — corner temporary incisors are erupting

2 years — permanent centrals / temporary lateral and corner teeth

3 years — the temporary incisors are worn

4 years — permanent central teeth / temporary lateral and corner incisors / central permanent incisors show wear

5 years — corner incisors meet in front only / central lateral and corner incisors all permanent

6 years — corner teeth now level / cup marks on all incisors can be seen

7 years — hook / the cup marks begin to fade

8 years — hook of corner teeth worn away / a dark line appears on the centrals

9 years — Galvayne's groove appears on corner teeth / dark line visible on all teeth

10 years — slope of teeth increases / the shape is more triangular, the cup marks less distinct

15 years — all teeth more triangular, cup marks have gone

20-25 years — Galvayne's groove is now at the base of the corner teeth and gradually disappearing

An excellent way of checking on the conformation and action of a new pony is to have him trotted out in hand. He should move forward smoothly, freely and willingly.

As showing and jumping classes usually restrict the height of ponies to 12.2 h.h. and under, 13.2 h.h. and under and 14.2 h.h. and under, ponies of 'odd' heights such as 12.3 h.h. or 14.3 h.h. are often cheaper to buy.

The certificate of warranty also describes the examined animal very carefully, and specific terms are used to describe colours and markings. Markings may be drawn on certifi-cates having outline sketches of a horse specially for the purpose. On other warranties, the markings are carefully described. Acquired marks, such as those resulting from injuries or operation scars, are also noted, as is the position of any irregular setting of the coat hairs in the form of whorls.

There are 'official' terms for describing the body colours of horses and ponies, and the principal colours recognised are bay, brown, black, grey and chestnut. Sometimes it is difficult to assess the true coat colour, but the hair of the muzzle and eyelids, along with the skin colour, can generally give the best indication of this.

Colours

Bay:
Is a rich bright brown colour which can vary in shade from a deep mahogany to a much lighter and more yellowish shade, approaching chestnut. A bay always has a black mane and tail, and frequently has black on the legs, when it is said to be bay with black points.

Bay-brown:
The predominating colour is brown, the muzzle is distinctly bay, and the points are all black.

Brown:
Can vary from a shade approaching bay, to nearly black. In doubtful cases, it is the colour on the muzzle that determines the animal's official colour. As in the bay, the brown is favoured if it has black points, although white markings are accepted on the face and legs.

Black:
The black pigmentation is uniform throughout the coat, limbs, mane and tail. The muzzle is also jet black. White markings are often on the face and sometimes the legs.

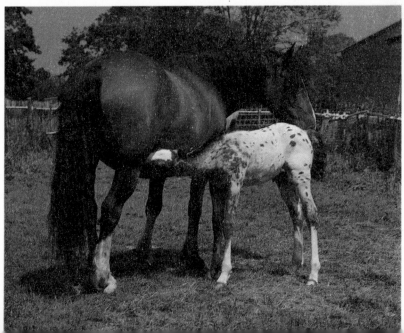

Bay ponies always have black manes and tails. This handsome bay mare was mated to an Appaloosa stallion to produce this striking and unusual bay spotted colt foal.

The bay-brown has a brown coat, a bay muzzle and a jet black mane and tail.

Brown is usually considered to be the smartest of all colours in the pony.

Chestnut:

Varies in colour from a rich burnished liver chestnut to a very pale yellow, with every conceivable shade in between. The true chestnut also has a chestnut mane and tail which, however, may be either lighter or

Right The true black is uniformly coloured all over except for permitted white markings.

Bright chestnut leading liver chestnut

darker than the coat colour. Very light chestnuts often have flaxen, blonde-coloured manes and/or tails. Most chestnuts have white facial markings and striking socks and stockings on the legs. The exception to this is the breed of heavy horse known as the Suffolk Punch, which is always a distinctive deep chestnut colour on its body, mane, tail and limbs, right down to its feet.

Cream:

A pale, even cream colour with an unpigmented skin. A rare colour, often complemented by a silver mane and tail. The eyes may be lacking in pigmentation and have a pale blue or pink appearance.

Dun:

A whole range of colours are known as dun. Blue-dun is a dilute black, and looks an attractive slate-blue in colour. Yellow-dun is a warm beige in tone, and golden-dun is a richer hue. Prehistoric horses were golden dun, and many of the dun horses and ponies seen today also exhibit the black spine line or eel stripe, plus

A true cream has a pale and unpigmented skin and often sports a silver mane and tail and light-coloured eyes.

the wither marks of their ancestors. The duns have black skin and generally have black points. Occasionally the legs show faint zebra markings.

Grey:

Comes in many varying shades. Greys are often born almost black

Dun ponies come in a wide range of shades. This Highland is a 'mouse' dun.

and lighten with age. Very old greys may appear pure white. The grey effect is produced by a mixture of black and white hairs and it is the variability of the mixtures which produce different effects. The dappled grey has circles of black hair all over the body and particularly concentrated on the quarters, rather like a child's rocking horse. The flea-bitten grey has dark specks of hair; its points may be either black or white.

Roan:
Is an interesting and striking colour range. In the strawberry or chestnut roan, the coat is a mixture of chestnut and white hairs. The blue-roan's coat is made up of black or black-brown with white, causing a bluish effect, and the bay or red-roan has a bay or bay-brown coat mixed with white.

Piebald:
In this colour the body is covered with large irregular patches of black and white.

Skewbald:
Is similarly marked to piebald but with white and any definite colour other than black.

Odd-coloured:
Is the term given to a horse or pony

27

The term 'grey' covers a range of colours from a dark steel grey through to a coat which appears pure white like that of this imposing Connemara stallion.

with a coat of large irregular patches of white and two other colours.

Body markings

Black marks:
Are small areas of black hairs among white or any other coloured hairs on the body.

Flecked:
A term to describe small areas of white hairs irregularly over the body. The coat can be termed 'heavily' or 'lightly' flecked.

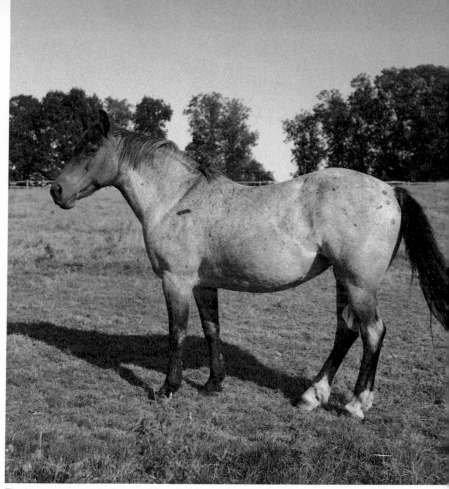
The bay roan coat of this pony is caused by a mixture of bay-brown and white hairs. The pony has a bay muzzle and the typically dark mane, tail and points of a true bay.

Grey-flecked:
Is when there are only a few white hairs present in the coat.

Patch:
A term used to describe any large and irregular area of hair which differs from the general body colour.

Spots:
Are small, practically circular collections of hairs which differ from the general body colour.

Flesh marks:
Are patches where the pigment of the skin is absent. They can often

be seen as paler marks in white areas.

Zebra marks:
Are stripes occasionally seen on the withers, neck, quarters or limbs.

Leg markings

White leg:
White area extends from hoof to above the knee or hock joint.

White stocking:
White area extends to knee or hock.

White sock:
White area extends to about half-way up the cannon bone.

White fetlock:
White area extends to the fetlock joint.

White pastern:
Pastern area downwards is white.

A piebald is white with black markings.

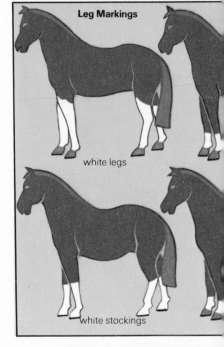

Leg Markings

white legs

white stockings

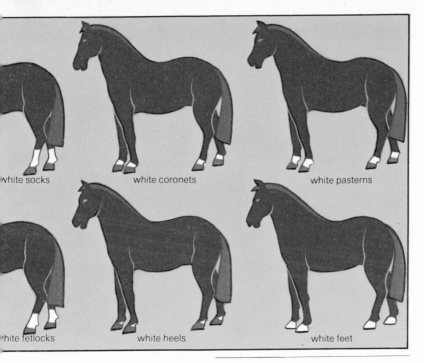

white socks   white coronets   white pasterns

white fetlocks   white heels   white feet

Left A strikingly marked skewbald pony.

White heel:
White hair at the heel only of a coloured leg.

White coronet:
White hair just above the hoof.

White foot:
A light hoof, usually a pinkish-yellow in colour and with a light sole.

Note: On a veterinary certificate, leg markings are generally described very accurately as, for example, 'white to half pastern,' and terms such as 'sock' and 'stocking' are not normally used.

Head markings

Star:
Is the name given to any white mark found on the forehead.

Stripe:
Is a narrow white marking down the face which does not extend past the flat anterior surface of the nasal bones. It may or may not be joined to a star, and is described according to its size and shape as 'broad', 'narrow', 'irregular', etc.

Blaze:
Is a white marking that covers practically the whole of the forehead between the eyes, and extends

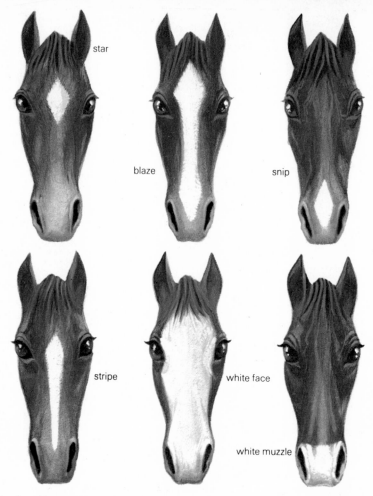

star

blaze

snip

stripe

white face

white muzzle

Head markings are named according to the location and extent of the white areas.

beyond the width of the nasal bones, usually as far as the muzzle.

White face:

Has the blaze effect extended over the whole forehead and the front of the face.

White muzzle:

A white area which covers both lips and extends to the nostrils.

Snip:

Is an isolated white marking situated between the nostrils.

Pedigree Ponies

Most ponies used for general riding purposes, and for instructing learners at a riding school, are crossbred animals. They are selected mainly for their suitability for the job, being of a useful height and having very quiet natures. Such ponies must be well-made and sound. They should have comfortable paces and be obedient to the aids. They must be willing to jump small obstacles, kind to ride, and very good in traffic. It is

This Arabian stallion is typical of those used as outcrosses in carefully-planned pony-breeding programmes. Infusion of Oriental blood has done much to refine native stock.

not really important whether or not they are beautiful to look at. For showing however, a pony's looks and conformation are of prime importance.

Pedigree ponies are those whose forebears are known and have been recorded for several generations. Pedigree ponies are usually registered with their relevant breed society, and their records are amended when they are sold to a new owner.

There are several British native breeds, popular all over the world, which are known collectively as Mountain and Moorland ponies. There are advantages in owning a pedigree pony, for it can be shown at all the large shows which have both ridden and in-hand classes. Many native ponies are as useful as they are beautiful and make excellent jumpers and gymkhana eventers. Thoroughbreds and Arabs are often crossed with native ponies to produce the elegant show ponies for their riding classes. And there are specialist breed shows for all manner of varieties including the spotted ponies and the Palominos.

A pedigree pony must conform to the standard of points laid down for the breed or type by its official society, which will always give help and advice to the novice.

	Bay	Black	Brown	Chestnut	Dun	Grey	Palomino	Roan	Piebald Skewbald
Caspian	o			o		o			
Connemara	o	o	o	o	o	P	o	o	
Dales	o	P	o			r			
Dartmoor	o	o	o	o	o	o		o	
Exmoor	o		o			o			
Fell	o	P	o		r	r			
Highland	o		o	o	o	o			
Lundy						P			
New Forest	o	o	o	o	o	o	o	o	o
Shetland	o	o	o	o	o	o		o	o
Welsh	o	o	o	o	o	o	o	o	

Key: o = accepted; P = predominant colour; r = rare

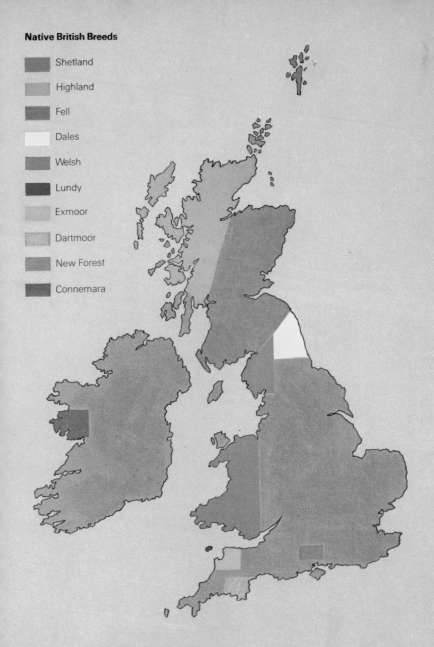

Native British Breeds

- Shetland
- Highland
- Fell
- Dales
- Welsh
- Lundy
- Exmoor
- Dartmoor
- New Forest
- Connemara

Connemara

Height:
13–14 hands (The English Connemara Society accepts ponies up to 14.2 hands).

Colour:
Grey is the most popular. Also bay, black, brown, dun with dorsal stripe and black points. Occasionally roan or chestnut.

Conformation:
Head – small and well balanced.

Eyes – large and expressive.

Ears – sharply cut, alert.

Neck – well-balanced, arched.

Shoulder – well-set, sloping.

Chest – good.

Back – short.

Legs – short with clean, hard, flat bone, and good hard feet.

Tail – long and flowing, set fairly high.

Action – free, straight and easy.

Overall appearance:
Alert, well-balanced pony, sturdy but graceful. Docile and hardy.

History:
The area from which the Connemara pony gets its name is in Connaught in western Ireland. It is a wild and beautiful region of mountains, lakes and marshes, which has been home to an indigenous breed of pony for many centuries. From these wild herds, today's Connemara has evolved, shaped by the elements and variable seasons into the tough and self-sufficient pony of today. It is often suggested that the original Connemara stock

came from the horses of a Spanish galleon wrecked off the coast in 1588. Others think the pony was present in Ireland before that date.

Certainly, rich merchants of Galway City, once a prosperous centre of trade and commerce, had dealings with Spain, and imported

superb Arabian and Barb horses.
It is likely that some imported stock
found its way to the neighbouring
district of Connemara and bred
with the native herds. There is
evidence of the Eastern influence in
the conformation and bearing of the
Connemara, but this is possibly due

The Connemara is a useful, general-
purpose pony; hardy and good-looking.

to more recent outcrosses, for
Arabian stallions were specially
acquired by estate owners during the
last century, and turned out with
the native mares.

The Dales

Height:
Up to 14.2 hands.

Colour:
Jet black, bay, brown and very occasionally grey.

Conformation:
Head – neat and pony-like.

Eyes – dark and kind.

Ears – small and neatly set.

Neck – short.

Shoulder – rather steep and straight.

Chest – strong with well-sprung ribs.

Back – wide and strong.

Legs – short and strong, good bone, and exceptional knees and hocks. Long, fine hair trims the fetlocks and the feet are of hard blue horn.

Tail – set rather low, of thick, curling hair.

Action – free walk, trots well, with rather high action.

Overall appearance:
Built like a small carthorse; a thickset and heavy pony giving the impression of strength and docility.

History:
For many years the Dales pony was used as a pack and harness pony to carry coal and lead from the mines of the north of England to the docks of Tyneside. The ponies travelled loose, in large droves, headed by a mounted man. Each carried about 100 kilograms (220 lbs) divided into two panniers.

They travelled at a steady walking pace covering about 380 kilo-

metres (240 miles) each week. With the introduction of railways which superseded pony transport, the number of Dales declined.

Later, the Dales pony proved its worth in agriculture, where its comparatively small size and sure-

A Dales pony mare with her enchanting newborn foal.

ness of foot made it the ideal work-horse for Yorkshire hill farms.

The army, noting the strength and versatility of the breed, chose the Dales for transporting heavy guns. Originally used only for draughtwork, the Dales is now in demand. Kind and placid by nature, this pony is as versatile as it is trustworthy, and makes an ideal ride-and-drive family pony.

The Dartmoor

Height:
Up to 12.2 hands.

Colour:
Preferably bay, black or brown. No other colour barred except piebald and skewbald. Excessive areas of white are discouraged.

Conformation:

Head – small and elegant.

Eyes – fairly large with kind expression.

Ears – small and alert.

Neck – medium length, strong.

Shoulder – well laid-back to slight withers.

Chest – plenty of heart-room, good deep girth.

Back – medium length, and strong.

Legs – straight with good hocks. The feet are tough and well shaped.

Tail – full and set high.

Action – low, straight and free moving.

Overall appearance:
An impression of great quality, that of a show hack or pony but without any exaggeration of action.

History:
For centuries the Dartmoor pony has survived the winter snows and gales on the forbidding, rock-strewn moors in the extreme south-west of England. Over the years, the breed has developed and been modified by the infusion of alien bloodlines.

First of all, invading Danes sailed up the River Tamar, and left behind stallions which found their way to the mares on the open moors.

Later, returning Crusaders brought Arabians and Barbs home with them, and these too have left their mark on the wild herds.

Until the mid 19th century the breed maintained a fairly uniform and recognisable type. With the advent of the Industrial Revolution, however, a scheme to breed pit ponies was conceived, and Shetland

A superb Dartmoor mare peacefully grazes with her confident colt foal.

stallions were released on to the moor. Type, size and quality rapidly deteriorated. Fortunately in 1899, a stud book was opened and programmes were put into action which saved the breed. Top quality Welsh Mountain stallions were used, as well as a fine Fell and a famous polo pony, and the excellent riding type was regained.

The breed became virtually extinct in 1943, for troops had trained on Dartmoor throughout the war years. Only swift and timely action by dedicated breeders saved the remaining stock, and today the Dartmoor is again well established.

The Exmoor

Height:
Stallions – up 12.3 hands.
Mares – up to 12.2 hands.

Colour:
Bay, brown or dun with black points. A 'mealy' muzzle is a breed characteristic of the Exmoor. It is a pale oatmeal colour and is also to be found around the eyes, on the stomach and between the thighs. Summer coat – close, soft and bright. Winter coat – harsh and wiry. There must be *no* white markings, not even a single white hair.

Conformation:
Head – small, clean cut with wide forehead.
Eyes – large, wide-set and prominent, often called 'toad eyes'.
Ears – short, thick and pointed.
Neck – good length of rein.
Shoulder: – clean, fine, well laid back.
Chest – deep, good heart-room, long, deep and well-sprung ribs.
Back – broad and level.
Legs – clean, short and straight, with neat, hard feet.
Tail – set well on.
Action – straight and smooth.

Overall appearance:
Alert expression and general poise. Balanced and symmetrical movement, and fine clean bone.

History:
By far the oldest of native British breeds, the Exmoor is believed to be truly indigenous, and to have been preserved, almost unchanged, since

prehistoric times. Once known as the Celtic pony, it was used as a pack animal, before being pressed into military service drawing the war chariots of the Celtic tribes. The wild tracts of land that extend from Somerset into Devon are sparsely

The hardy Exmoor and her foal exhibit 'mealy' muzzles typical of their breed.

populated, and ponies run wild and free over the bleak windswept moorlands. In winter, the grazing is poor and the Exmoor pony has a lean time. The harsh conditions have ensured that only the strongest and hardiest of the breed has survived, and over the generations the Exmoor has come to be regarded as an outstanding pony for both stamina and strength.

The Fell

Height:
13–14 hands.

Colour:
Usually black, sometimes brown or bay and very occasionally grey. White markings are not favoured, but a small star or a little white on the heels is acceptable.

Conformation:

Head – small, pony-like with wide forehead and strong cheekbones.

Eyes – bright, prominent and intelligent.

Ears – small, neat and well-formed.

Neck – long and strong.

Shoulder – well laid-back, sloping.

Chest – strong and muscular.

Back – broad and strong with a good outline.

Legs – short and strong with good bone and excellent knees and hocks. 'Feather' on the fetlocks is a feature of the breed, and their feet are of hard, blue horn.

Tail – full and of curled hair, set high and carried gaily.

Action – good walk, well-balanced trot, shows great pace and good knee and hock action.

Overall appearance:
An alert businesslike pony of utility type. Very long and curly mane and tail, and fine hair trimming the fetlocks. Sweet, gentle expression.

History:
The Fell and the Dales were once a common breed descended from the ancient Celtic pony. The high ridges of the Pennine chain of hills down

the centre of the north of England effectively divided the pony herds and those to the east developed as the rounder, larger Dales, while the type bred on the west side chiefly in Cumbria was known as the Fell.

The gentle, sweet-natured Fell pony responds willingly to her rider's aids.

It is thought that the Romans, considering the native British ponies to be too small for haulage work, imported powerful black Friesian horses which measured 15 hands and were exceptional trotters. It is possible that these interbred with native stock and formed the basis of the Fell breed of today.

The Highland

Height:
From about 13 to 14.2 hands.
Colour:
A wide range of coat colours is found in the Highland pony. It may be black, brown or grey and occasionally bay or liver chestnut, perhaps especially eyecatching and sporting a silver mane and tail. The original colour is the yellow dun, but there are other attractive and unusual dun colours which are a feature of this breed. A distinctive dorsal eel stripe is often present in Highlands. Apart from a star, white markings are discouraged.

Conformation:
Head – well carried, broad, but short between eyes and muzzle.
Eyes – intelligent and kind.

The Highland stallions, with their beautifully crested necks and full flowing manes and tails, are always a great draw in the Mountain and Moorland sections of shows.

The Highland's strength enables it to carry a stag even over rough terrain.

Ears – short and well-set.
Neck – strong, not short, arched crest, long flowing mane.
Shoulder – well set back.
Chest – deep and strong.
Back – short, with slight natural curve.
Legs – flat bone, strong, broad knees and hocks, broad feet.
Tail – strong, carried gaily and well-set.
Action – free and straight.
Overall appearance:
Sound, strong and heavy, but of typically pony type. Beautiful head points to influence of Arabian forebears.
History:
The Highland is a breed of great antiquity, thought to be descended from the horses of northern Asia that moved westwards after the last great Ice Age. Having been isolated on separate islands, the breed developed along different lines, and three distinct types emerged. The smallest, from Barra and the outer islands of the Hebrides, averaging 13 hands high, is the original Highland pony. The Scottish Riding pony is larger and was developed from the smaller strain by judicious outcrossing. The massive Mainland pony is the type now generally recognised as the Highland, and is a very strong, docile pony capable of carrying heavy loads for long periods over difficult going.

47

The Lundy

Height:
An average of 13.2 hands.

Colour:
Preferably dun, but all other colours are acceptable except piebald, skewbald and albino.

Conformation and overall appearance:
The Lundy pony is attractive and of true pony character. It must be hardy, surefooted and active to survive the rigours of the winter weather on the high granite plateau of the island on which it is bred.

Well-made, with an attractive head and kind, intelligent eye, the Lundy pony is full of quality and substance and is a fine, natural jumper. It is possessed of a remarkably kind temperament, is keenly intelligent and very bold.

History:
In 1929, 42 New Forest mares were shipped out from the Devon coast to Lundy Island, where they were off-loaded into the sea and encouraged to swim ashore. There is no harbour or quay on Lundy, merely a small landing beach and a long, climbing cliff path to the plateau.

Several stallions were tried with the mares, with varying degrees of success, and eventually the Lundy pony became standardised. In 1971 the National Pony Society visited the herd and advised on the welfare and selective breeding of the ponies, in order that they might be granted recognition for registration purposes.

Mares approved by the experts were branded with the official Lundy Flag mark, and all other stock was sold. Since then all approved stock has been branded with the Flag emblem and also alphabetically, indicating the year of birth, and

A product of its tough environment, the Lundy pony is kind, intelligent and bold.

numerically, indicating the order of birth. Thus the first approved foal born in 1972 was branded 'A.1.', the second 'A.2.', and so on. In 1976, the breed had its first specialist class at the National Pony Show, and in 1977 Lundy Island started a register of approved Lundy ponies.

Rare in numbers and in its outstanding qualities, the Lundy pony is an admirable and attractive pony.

The New Forest

Height:
12–14.2 hands.

Colour:
Any, except skewbald and piebald, but usually bay or brown.

Conformation:

Head – large, but Eastern type.

Eyes – dark and kind.

Ears – short and pricked.

Neck – short.

Shoulder – good and sloping.

Chest – deep with good depth of girth.

Back – short, narrow, leading to rather drooping quarters.

Legs – straight, short and strong with good feet.

Tail – set fairly low.

Action – good, coming from the shoulder and not the knee – very surefooted and safe ride.

Overall appearance:
Really neat, compact pony of diverse type.

History:
Ponies have inhabited the thousands of hectares (or acres) known as the New Forest since the reign of King Canute. Situated in Hampshire, north of Southampton, it is wildly beautiful with woodlands and great tracts of open, heather-covered commonland. Though quite free to roam at will, the New Forest pony is very territorial in its habits.

It lives in small groups, usually several generations of the same family, and grazes a particular area. The pony's grazing territory is

known as its haunt, and encompasses feeding grounds, shelter and a watering place. Although it lives in the semi-wild state, each New Forest pony has an owner, and carries a brand or tail marking to signify that ownership. Annual round-ups or drifts are organised by the forest agisters – overseers appointed to look after the welfare of all the forest

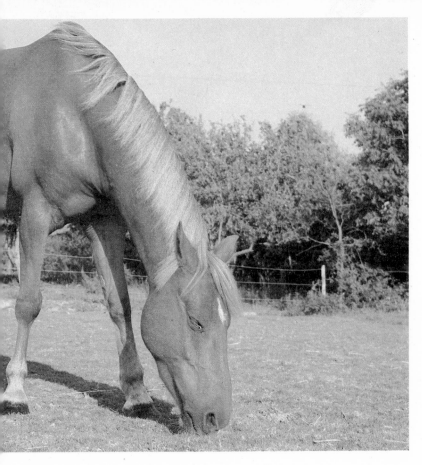

The New Forest makes an excellent riding pony for children and light adults.

animals. At the round-up, which is performed by expert riders on local ponies, the herds are collected into wooden compounds. The owners of the ponies take this opportunity to examine their ponies, to worm them and to administer any other necessary medications. The foals which are to be sold are singled out, and the rest are tail-marked or branded.

The introduction of many different stallions to the Forest over the generations has produced a very heterogeneous breed, but the New Forest pony of today has definite breed characteristics of substance, strength and versatility.

The Shetland

Height:
Shetlands are measured in centimetres and inches, not hands. They must not exceed 101.6 centimetres (40 inches) at 3 years and 106.6 centimetres (42 inches) at 4 years and over.

Colour:
Black or any other known colour.

Conformation:
Head – small and well-shaped.
Eyes – wide apart, kind and intelligent.
Ears – short, well-placed.
Neck – strong and muscular, with a good crest in stallions.
Shoulder – well-laid and oblique.
Chest – broad and strong.
Back – short and with broad, strong quarters.
Legs – short, strong and well-muscled, with good bone and springy pasterns. Feet open, round, tough.
Tail – set fairly low, very full and long, often sweeping the ground.
Action – free and true, very gay and light in harness as well as under saddle.

Overall appearance:
Small and appealing pony with an impression of great strength for its diminutive size.

History:
Records of the pony's existence in the Shetland Islands, in the north of Scotland, date back many centuries. It has been thought that the breed's tiny size is due mainly to lack of feed and the severe climate in

which it evolved. This is unlikely to be true, as specimens of the breed raised for generations in kind weather conditions and given ample keep, still retain their small stature. It is much more likely that very small animals were easier to ship to remote islands, to help with the agricultural work, in the days before

With a history of employment in the pits, today's Shetlands can enjoy the sunshine.

sophisticated winches and lifting gear were known. Thus small ponies were selected and bred small stock. The harsh environment of the islands probably caused the Shetland to grow its unique double, and virtually waterproof, winter coat.

In 1847, with the coming of the Industrial Revolution, many Shet-lands were used as pit ponies, their small size and immense strength making them perfect for work underground. Nowadays they are in great demand as children's pets and for riding and harness work.

Characteristics of the Welsh Ponies & Cobs

Section:	Welsh Mountain Pony 'A'	Welsh Pony 'B'	Welsh Pony of Cob Type 'C'	Welsh Cob 'D'
Height:	Up to 12 hands	Up to 13.2 hands	Up to 13.2 hands	Over 13.2 hands
Overall appearance:	Looks well-bred with concave face similar to Arabian horses. A very neat and typical pony breed.	A definite riding pony type full of quality and substance.	Sturdy, strong and active with pony character.	Sturdy and strong, heavily-built but retaining pony character. Spectacular at the trot.
Conformation: Head	small and elegant, clean-cut.		typical pony head – roman nose deemed a fault.	
Eyes	bold and kind, wide-set.		bold, prominent and set wide apart.	
Ears	small and sharp, set high on head.		small and alertly carried.	
Neck	good length, arched.		lengthy, carried well. Strong crest in stallions.	
Shoulder	long and well-sloped.		strong and well laid-back.	
Chest	deep with good girth and well-sprung ribs.		strong with deep girth and good heart-room.	
Back	fairly short, strong, with good loins and quarters.		muscular, short and strong.	
Legs	fine, with good hocks, sloping pasterns and well-shaped feet.		fairly short, strong and muscular. May have lightly feathered fetlocks. Feet exceptionally hard.	
Action:	Swift and free, straight from the shoulder. Uses hocks well and carries head high.	Smooth and fluid – the perfect action for a riding pony with the hocks well under the body.	Free, true and forcible. The knee is bent and the whole foreleg is extended straight from the shoulder in the characteristic trot. Very showy and active at all paces.	
Colour:	Any colour is permitted in all sections *except* piebald and skewbald.			

The Welsh

To the novice the most confusing of all native pony breeds must be the Welsh. There are four quite different types of Welsh pony; each has its own characteristics, and its own separate section in the Welsh Stud Book.

SECTION A – the Welsh
                   Mountain pony
SECTION B – The Welsh pony
SECTION C – the Welsh pony of
                   Cob Type
SECTION D – the Welsh Cob

All the Welsh have certain features in common, regardless of their section. They are all possessed of excellent temperament and are highly intelligent. All possess courage and stamina, and they all have great jumping ability.

History:

The Welsh Mountain pony has the oldest recorded history of all the British native pony breeds. Julius Caesar, it is said, founded a stud on the shores of Lake Bala, in Wales. He used some imported Oriental horses to modify the native hill type, and

The intelligent Welsh Mountain pony (Section A) has a slightly dished head inherited from its Arab ancestors.

A perfect riding pony with good bone, the Welsh pony (Section B) is ideal for children's show and performance classes, and usually shows ability as a jumper.

the stock was in great demand for riding and for pack carrying. It is thought that Welsh Mountain mares were later used in the development of the English Thoroughbred. It is certain that this mountain breed has played a major role in the production of the polo pony and the hackney. Welsh mares were introduced to the New Forest in the 13th century to strengthen that breed, and also contributed significantly to the improvement of the Dartmoor herds.

At the close of the last century, systematic efforts were made to preserve the essential characteristics of the Welsh Mountain pony, and the success of the scheme is reflected in the popularity of the four types of Welsh seen today. The Sections B, C and D animals are all descended from the Welsh Mountain pony and are different types rather than different breeds. It is true to say that any rider could quite easily find a perfect mount within the Welsh breed alone.

The Welsh pony of Cob Type (Section C) must not exceed 13.2 hands but it is very strong and compact, suitable for riding and harness work, and is very showy.

The Welsh Cob (Section D) exceeds 13.2 hands and is a strong, hardy animal. His typically pony character makes him very versatile and an excellent hunter.

The Appaloosa & Spotted

Height:
Any; Appaloosa 14.2–15.2 in U.S.A.
Colour:
Spotted patterns including:
Leopard spotted – Spots of any colour on a white or light background;
Blanket spotted – A white rump or back on which are spots of any colour;
Snowflake – White spots on a background of any colour.
(It is usual to find silver hair in the mane and tail.)
Conformation:
Variable, but preferably of quality riding type.
History:
Spotted horses have been known since ancient times and have been recorded all over the world. In Ancient China they were considered sacred, and known as 'Heavenly Horses'. First imported by Emperor Wu Ti in about 100 B.C. they were popular subjects in Chinese art for centuries and were much prized by the ruling classes. Emperor Hsuan t'sung is reputed to have owned many spotted horses among the 40,000 in his stables.

In 400 B.C. a famous warrior, Rustan, rode his spotted horse Rakush into battle, and the pair went down in history as indomitable fighters. Legend has it that all the spotted horses in Persia are direct descendants of this mighty warhorse.

In Britain, spotted steeds are depicted on many documents and manuscripts dating from the 12th century. A picture of King Richard II in a manuscript of 1397 shows one of his retinue riding a chestnut spotted horse. The Spanish Jennet was a popular import during the early 18th century and it is likely that some of the spotted horses and ponies of today are descended from these. A very fine spotted horse is the subject of *Lady Conway's Spanish Jennet*, an English painting of 1700.

The Appaloosa is derived from the Palouse area of Idaho, U.S.A., where it was developed by the Nez Percé Indians from horses introduced by Spanish invaders. Its black or chocolate spots can be felt by touch, as they appear in relief on the fine coat of this breed.

Klaus, a superbly marked and famous leopard-spotted Appaloosa stallion.

In Denmark, during the 19th century a spotted mare was mated and produced a similarly spotted foal. The breeder owned the Knab- strup estate, and named the new breed after this. Knabstrupper horses are famed for their hardiness and powers of endurance.

The Appaloosa has a pink skin with dark spots superimposed on a silky white coat.

The Caspian

Height:

11–12 hands.

Colour:

Bay, grey or chestnut with occasional white markings on the face and legs.

Conformation:

Head – short and fine with pronounced forehead and small muzzle.

Eyes – large and lustrous.

Ears – very short.

Neck – graceful, carried well and arched.

Shoulders – well sloped, to good withers.

Chest – good.

Back – straight, fairly short.

Legs – dense strong bone. A feature is the extremely strong, oval hoof. This pony doesn't need to be shod even when working on stony ground.

Tail – set high, flowing.

Action – long walk, and a long swinging trot with a natural, far-reaching action. The canter is smooth, and the gallop very fast and flat. The Caspian enjoys its ability to jump high and accurately.

Overall appearance:

This pony looks like a small and well-proportioned horse.

History:

At present the natural home of the Caspian is along the shoreline of the Caspian sea, where it is known as the Mouleki or Pouseki pony. It is probable, however, that its original

A Caspian mare and a map of the area where the Caspian was discovered.

home, thousands of years ago, was in an area of West Iran. It is thought that the Caspian pony may well have been the ancestor of the Arabian horse. It is certainly a breed of great antiquity and of untainted bloodlines. Characteristics shared by both Arabian and Caspian horses are the vaulted forehead, fine bone and exceptionally dense hoof.

The Seal of Darius the Great, 500 B.C., now in the British Museum, shows a pair of tiny horses, of typical Caspian structure, pulling the royal chariot on a lion hunt.

Only in the last few years have pure Caspian ponies been brought from Iran, and breeding herds are well established in U.S.A., Bermuda and Britain. Already the Caspian has found favour as the perfect child's pony, being so well-made, narrow, but with substance, and with a delightful temperament.

The Haflinger

Height:
About 14 hands.
Colour:
Dark chestnut with a flaxen or lighter coloured mane and tail. White markings are permitted.
Conformation:
Head – heavy but not coarse.
Eyes – large and alert.
Ears – small and pricked.
Neck – short and strong.
Shoulder – powerful and well laid-back.
Chest – deep and strong.

Back – short and broad.
Legs – short and powerful with strong joints, plenty of bone and good, hard feet.
Tail – long and full, set well on.
Action – steady, powerful and sure-footed, with low head carriage while climbing slopes.
Overall appearance:
Brightly coloured, sturdy, giving an impression of strength and safety.

History:

Originally bred in the South Tyrol, the Haflinger is a small, strong and typical mountain breed, originally developed as a pack animal. Its appearance shows the influence of early Arabian bloodlines, however, and the breed is often described as being a 'prince in front and a peasant behind'.

In and around the mountain

Haflingers play in their snow-covered paddock, warm in their winter coats.

regions of its birth, the Haflinger has been used for many years to haul timber and hay, and to pull sleighs during the winter. Its surefootedness has made it a popular breed for trekking and riding centres and its good action makes it a safe, comfortable ride for all age groups.

The Palomino

Note: This is really a colour type, not a breed; however, these ponies have a place in the present and a long history.

Height:
In the U.S.A. the Palomino varies from 14.2–15.3 hands. In Britain, there are classes at shows for Palomino stock of all types and heights.

Colour:
The body colour is like that of a freshly-minted gold coin, with a mane and tail of pure white hair. There must not be more than 15 per cent of coloured hairs in either the mane or tail, and the coat must not show any signs of dark or white spots, a dorsal line or zebra stripes. White markings are permitted on the face and legs. The skin is dark.

Conformation:
As there are Palomino Welsh, Palomino Shetlands, Palomino part-Arabians and so on, the conformation must be ideal for each particular breed. In breeding for this elusive colour, quality of stock is vital, for foals may be born without the desired golden coats and will only be valuable as riding horses and ponies if of high quality.

Palomino foals are pale cream at birth and gradually darken with age. The Palomino grows a pale winter coat and only regains its guinea-gold appearance in spring.

History:
The Palomino colouring is thought to have originated in Spain, and was

known as Ysabella or Isabella, being named after the queen who did so much to encourage exploration during the latter half of the fifteenth century.

64

The ancient Greeks described their chariot horses as *xanthos*, and shining like the sun. This colouring is usually translated as dun or chestnut, but it is possible that they, too, were Palomino, for there is no colour that glows more golden.

A gloriously golden Palomino contrasts starkly with her palely immature foal.

All about Tack

When man first started to ride he soon realised the importance of having control over his horse, and slipped a loop of rope around its lower jaw in order to stop and guide the animal at will. Eventually more sophisticated bridles were developed, and by the seventh century B.C. Assyrian soldiers rode horses equipped with metal bits held in place by bridles of leather straps and thongs.

Xenophon, the great horseman and writer who lived in Ancient Greece during the fourth century B.C. described the art of using curb and plain bits in conjunction, just as we do today with a modern double bridle.

Bridles were in use long before saddles were invented. Pads of cloth were often tied on the horses' backs to give their riders more comfort on long journeys. As time passed, these pads were quilted and shaped for better fit, and straps of various types were designed to prevent them from slipping forwards or back.

The first stirrups were merely loops of rope, woven cloth or leather, laid across the saddle pads to support the rider's feet.

As the horse was used mainly in battle, it quickly became apparent that the secure seat of the rider and his control over the horse were of paramount importance. Craftsmen, skilled in the art of making harness and accoutrements for draught and chariot use, were employed to create efficient saddles and bridles for riding and military purposes.

In the Middle Ages, heavier horses were used in battle, and the saddles, bridles and bits were also heavier and more clumsy in appearance. Saddlery at that time was something of a status symbol, and the

A warhorse and rider of the Middle Ages, protected by heavy, cumbersome armour

equipment was often lavishly tooled and embellished. As time passed, leather proved itself to be the best material for tack for its qualities of strength and durability. Various metals were used to make the many designs of bits.

Saddles and bridles have evolved gradually, and today they are made in light, supple leather in various designs, each with a specific purpose. It is very important to choose the correct tack, and to ensure that it fits the pony perfectly.

Essential equipment

Certain basic equipment is essential for general riding purposes and is known as saddlery or 'tack'.

First of all there is the saddle, which must have a girth to hold it in place, and a pair of stirrup leathers which hold the stirrup irons. Then a bridle with a snaffle bit attached, complete with reins and noseband. Finally, a halter or head collar, with rope, in order to catch, lead and tie up the pony.

Good leather is expensive, and the making of tack is a highly-skilled job, so it follows that good quality saddlery will be expensive. If properly treated, however, it will last for many years in excellent condition. Secondhand tack which has been maintained in good condition will be soft and supple, comfortable for both pony and rider if correctly fitted, and it looks better than new tack. A knowledgeable person should check the saddlery before purchase to make sure that there are no weak places in the leatherwork which could break under stress.

It is quite usual for ponies to be sold complete with their own well-fitting saddlery. Otherwise the basic equipment can be bought from advertisements in newspapers and magazines, or by contacting local pony or riding clubs which often have lists of tack for sale. Saddlery shops usually carry stocks of second-hand as well as new equipment, and

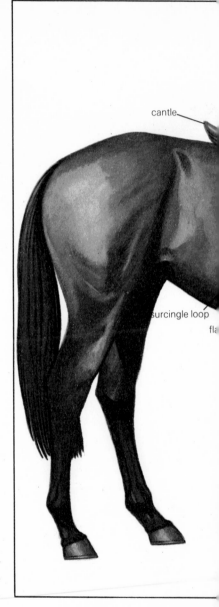

cantle

surcingle loop

fla

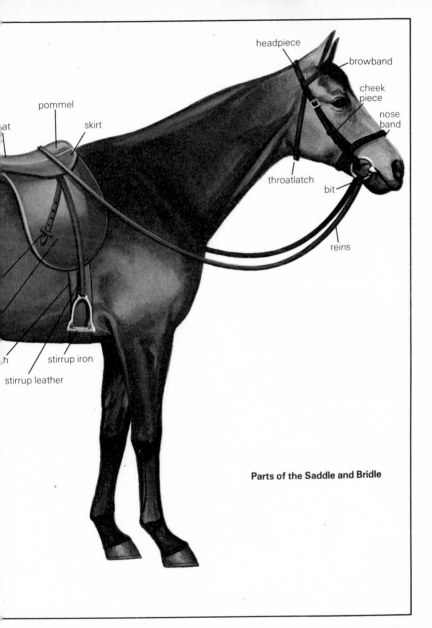

headpiece

browband

cheek piece

nose band

pommel

skirt

at

throatlatch

bit

reins

h

stirrup iron

stirrup leather

Parts of the Saddle and Bridle

the staff are trained to advise on the correct fitting of saddles and bridles, and the choice of bits.

It is a great mistake to try to economise on costs by buying cheap tack. Good leather is well worth its extra cost in terms of long service, comfort and safety. Cracked leather can break at a critical moment, and broken reins, bridles and girths can cause fatal accidents. Shabby old saddles of strong, supple leather are far superior to some of the flashy new saddles, made of weak, split leather which are offered for sale at 'bargain' prices. Good tack is expensive, but your life may depend on it.

Types of saddle

There are many types of saddle for

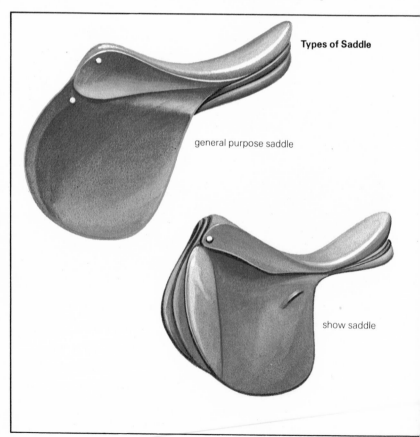

Types of Saddle

general purpose saddle

show saddle

the specialist rider, from the tiny lightweight racing saddle at one extreme, to the elaborate Western show saddle at the other. Halfway between these two extremes comes the General Purpose saddle, which is, as its name suggests, ideal for all normal riding purposes. The framework on which a saddle is built is known as the tree, and is traditionally made of beechwood. The shape of the tree determines the finished shape of the saddle and the depth of its seat. Most general purpose saddles have a deep central seat which encourages the rider both to sit well and to have good contact with the horse's back.

The deepest seat is found in a saddle made on a spring tree which has two strips of light steel stretched along the underside of the tree,

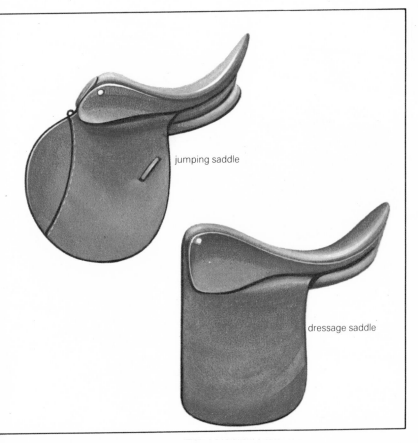

jumping saddle

dressage saddle

giving greater flexibility and therefore better contact between horse and rider. The general purpose saddle can be used for most types of riding, including schooling the young pony, hacking, preliminary jumping, gymkhana events and hunting. For more specialised work it is best to invest in the correct saddle for the job.

Those who intend to do a lot of show-jumping for example, should buy a Jumping saddle. This allows for a forward riding position, and often has shaped and padded knee rolls to help the rider to maintain the correct position through the jumping sequence. A jumping saddle is not satisfactory for everyday use, as its design can give the pony a sore back when the rider's weight is in the normal riding position for long periods, instead of being forward, and on the knees.

For showing and dressage, saddles with very straight cut flaps are used, The Show saddle is cut to fit the back of the pony very closely and the straight flaps are designed to show off the animal's shoulders to their best advantage. The whole purpose of such a saddle is to enhance the appearance of the pony, rather than to aid the rider in any way.

A Dressage saddle has a deep seat with flaps and bars so positioned

A saddle must fit really well to prevent the development of a sore back or galls.

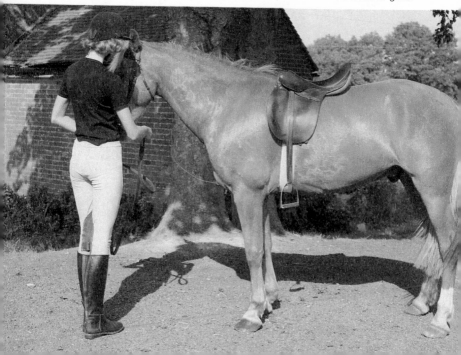

that the rider's legs are free to give the subtle aids necessary for this advanced work.

Fitting the saddle

It is very important that the saddle fits both the pony and the rider. It is very uncomfortable to ride on a saddle that is too small, for the rider's weight goes too far back and the legs have an insufficient amount of flap on which to grip. Too large a saddle allows the rider to roll around in it and can give the pony saddle sores. When buying a saddle, expert advice should be sought, and the saddle should be tried out for size, preferably on a pony. Saddles are measured from pommel to cantle, but vary in design so that it does not always follow that a 40-centimetre (16-inch) saddle that fits you well at the riding school will correspond entirely with the 40-centimetre (16-inch) saddle advertised in the Press.

Having found a saddle to fit yourself, it must be fitted on your pony. It is imperative that daylight can be seen through the gullet from back to front when the saddle is fitted and someone is mounted. There should be room to insert four fingers between the pommel and the pony's withers. When fitting a new saddle for the first time it is a good idea to put a thick folded blanket on the pony, then the saddle, before girthing up and riding around for half an hour.

Then, when the saddle is re-moved, the impression shows whether or not it fits correctly on the muscles on either side of the spine. Saddles can be altered by being restuffed, but the shape of the tree is permanent. Many people use a saddle pad or numnah under an ill-fitting saddle, but this often has a very detrimental effect on the pony's back and also lessons the rider's contact with his mount.

If a pony has poor withers or shoulders, a crupper may be fitted to prevent the saddle slipping forward. The crupper is a leather loop which goes around the pony's tail and straps on to the rear of the saddle. Ponies with weak quarters can have a leather breast-plate around the chest to prevent the saddle slipping back.

Check-list for fitting a saddle
1 It must not press on loins or withers.
2 It must not touch the spine.
3 Front panel must clear shoulders.
4 The front arch must not pinch the withers.

Saddles – how they are made

To have a perfectly fitting saddle it is necessary to have one specially made to measure by a saddler, and this is far too expensive for the average pony owner. To make a saddle, the saddler first measures the pony by using a thin strip of soft, pliable lead. He places this over the pony's back at the point where the saddle pommel fits, and moulds the lead gently against the firm muscles. The lead strip is carefully removed, laid on a sheet of paper, and the shape is traced off. The seat and cantle points are also moulded and traced, and measurements of the rider's length of leg are used to determine the size of the slaps and seat.

Making the wooden saddle tree is a highly-skilled job, and when it is completed it is covered, first with webbing and then with a serge foundation. The saddle seat is fashioned from thin pigskin which is an exceptionally hardwearing leather that does not stretch or distort in use. Steel stirrup bars are fitted to the tree, and then covered with small skirts of cowhide sewn into the seat. The large saddle flaps are also fashioned from cowhide, and their shape is dictated by the use to which the saddle will be put.

The panels are skilfully made next, and fitted to the front arch of the saddle, then the girth straps are fixed to the tree. They are perhaps the most vital part of the saddle from the safety aspect. They must be very strong and very securely fitted.

To finish off the saddle, leather guards are fitted which cover the

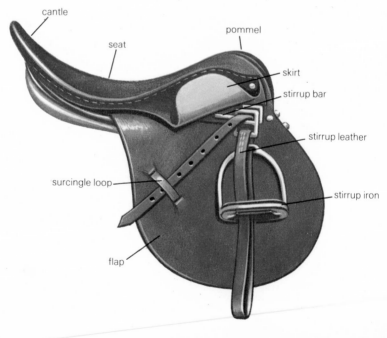

cantle

seat

pommel

skirt

stirrup bar

stirrup leather

stirrup iron

surcingle loop

flap

girth buckles, and prevent them marking and wearing the underside of the flaps.

Saddles must be treated with care. When removed from the pony, they should be placed in a safe position. If a pony rolls with his saddle on, or treads on a saddle left carelessly on the ground, the tree may be broken and the saddle cannot be used until it is repaired. If the saddle has to be placed on the ground, it should stand up on the pommel and not be left in a spread-eagled heap. To carry a saddle, place it over your

Saddles are expensive and should be treated with care. The easiest way to carry a saddle is to rest it over your bent arm.

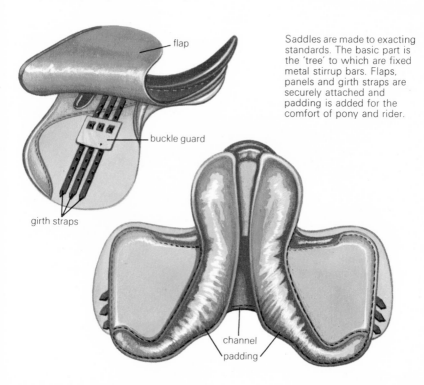

Saddles are made to exacting standards. The basic part is the 'tree' to which are fixed metal stirrup bars. Flaps, panels and girth straps are securely attached and padding is added for the comfort of pony and rider.

flap

buckle guard

girth straps

channel

padding

arm with the front arch in the crook of your elbow. Never allow the saddle lining to become encrusted with sweat and dust; and keep the leatherwork clean and supple at all times. A good saddle is essential for good riding. It is the most expensive single piece of equipment that you require but, with care, will last many years.

Girths

There are four main types of girth available: leather, string, webbing and nylon. The girth is merely a strap designed to hold the saddle securely in place, and is fitted with strong buckles.

As a pony in soft condition is likely to get galls when rubbed by a badly-fitting girth, it is important to check the fit and condition of the girth every time it is used. The best girths are made of leather but these are also the most expensive. The Three-fold, made of baghide, is usually handsewn with two rustproof buckles at either end. This is ideal for general use and schooling. For more active pursuits such as hunting or jumping the Fitzwilliam is often used. Also of baghide, it has extra buckles. The Balding and Atherstone are shaped girths, and prevent chafing during fast exercise. Some girths have elastic insets at the ends, some are all elastic, and these are useful in allowing the animal to breathe more easily after great exertion, such as eventing.

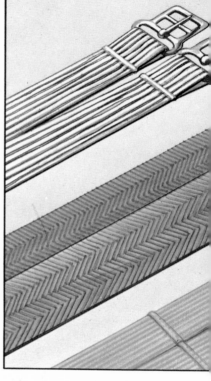

For show use, a Tubular Linen girth is used. This consists of two pieces of white linen, overlapped in the centre and the join lined with pimpled rubber which prevents the girth from slipping.

A Lampwick girth is ideal for summer use, being very soft, light and strong and fairly inexpensive.

Webbing girths are made in various qualities and the better ones wear well. They are made with a single buckle at either end and must be used in pairs. They soon become

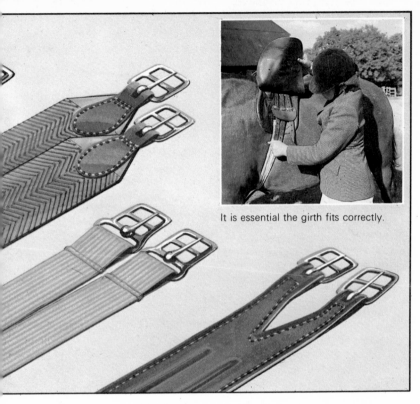

It is essential the girth fits correctly.

Types of girth, from top to bottom: string, webbing, nylon and leather.

hard with sweat and need regular washing to keep them serviceable.

Perhaps the cheapest form of girth is the Nylon Cord. This is made of very strong nylon strands and is tough, easy to wash and prevents chafing. The main drawback to this type of girth is the necessity in its design for large clumsy buckles which are often of poor quality and can damage the saddle. To protect the inside of the saddle flap a pair of Girth Safes can be purchased. These are leather shields which slide over the girth straps and are adjusted to rest over the buckles.

Whatever kind of girth is used, it must fit correctly, and buckle firmly three or four holes up the girth straps on either side of the saddle when you are mounted. Girths must be kept scrupulously clean with well-oiled buckles, and the girth straps of the saddle kept supple and free from cracks or weakness.

Stirrups

Stirrup leathers are made from cow hide, rawhide or buffalo hide and, when new, will stretch a little. For this reason, a new pair of leathers should be alternated from side to side. Most riders tend to place more weight in one stirrup than the other, and it is important to stretch out the pair of leathers evenly. The greatest wear on a stirrup leather comes on the area which passes through the iron, and it is advisable to adjust the length of the leathers by a hole or two occasionally, so that the wear is evened out. The holes in the leathers may become stretched or enlarged, and these, and the stitching at the buckle end, should be checked constantly for signs of deterioration.

Stirrup irons should be made of stainless steel or a nickel mixture. Solid nickel irons are available but they break easily and may cause a severe accident. It is very important to select irons of the right size, about three centimetres (one inch) wider than the widest part of your riding footwear. The iron must be large enough to allow the foot to come clear if the rider falls but it must not be so large that the foot could slip right through and become trapped.

The Kournakoff stirrup iron was invented by a Russian cavalry officer, and is designed to fix the position of the foot with the toe up, heel down and the outside edge of the sole higher than the inside edge. With the foot held in this position,

Four different types of stirrup iron.

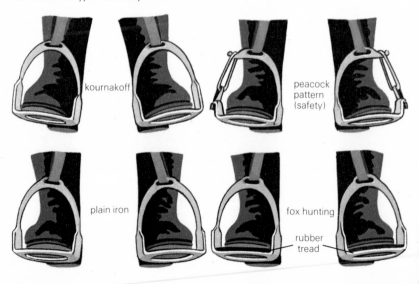

kournakoff

peacock pattern (safety)

plain iron

fox hunting

rubber tread

the knee and thigh of the rider are held inwards against the saddle, giving an excellent riding position. These irons are clearly marked 'left' and 'right' and must not be used on the wrong sides of the saddle.

Safety irons have gone slowly out of fashion over the years, although the Peacock Pattern iron is still used quite widely for children. The safety iron consists of three metal sides including the tread and the remaining side is formed from a strong rubber ring stretched between a hook and a stud. Should the rider fall, the ring detaches and frees the foot. The Plain iron is the design most commonly used today, and is of a standard pattern. For hunting it may be fitted with a rubber tread to give grip to the sole of the riding boot.

Types of bridle

Bridles are usually advertised in three sizes – pony-, Cob- or full-size. Many ponies have large heads and require cob-size bridles. There are five groups of bridle named after the bit used: the Snaffle, the Weymouth, the Pelham, the Gag and the Bitless, and all types can be classified under one of these groups. The basic components of the bridle are common to all five groups, even if slightly modified.

It is most important that you learn about the various parts of the bridle and how they fit together correctly, for they should be taken apart after use for thorough cleaning before being reassembled.

First, there is the headpiece which goes over the top of the pony's head and in which is incorporated the throatlatch. The throatlatch passes under the pony's throat and is buckled up fairly loosely, but just tightly enough to prevent the bridle coming off over the pony's head in the event of an accident. The browband which goes round the pony's forehead, under the forelock, slots on to the headpiece. Joined on to the two sides of the headpiece are the short, straight cheekpieces, which, in turn are buckled on to the bit.

The noseband is quite separate, and this has a long narrow strap which is passed up and under the cheek pieces, through the browband, under the headpiece and then buckles on the nearside of the face. The noseband itself passes under the cheek pieces and is buckled behind the chin. The leather reins are buckled to the bit rings on either side.

For general riding, a Snaffle bridle is commonly used, which has a single rein. The Double bridle has a curb chain which fits in the chin groove, and a fine leather chinstrap to keep the chain in place. These bridles have two reins, the top rein raises the pony's head and makes it flex its jaw to the bit; while correct use of the curb rein encourages the pony to arch his neck and to get his hocks under him in a collected manner.

Specially stitched and sewn bridles are used for showing classes, and substantially made bridles are generally employed for hunting.

Bitless bridles, or Hackamores, must only be used by the most experienced of riders with secure seats

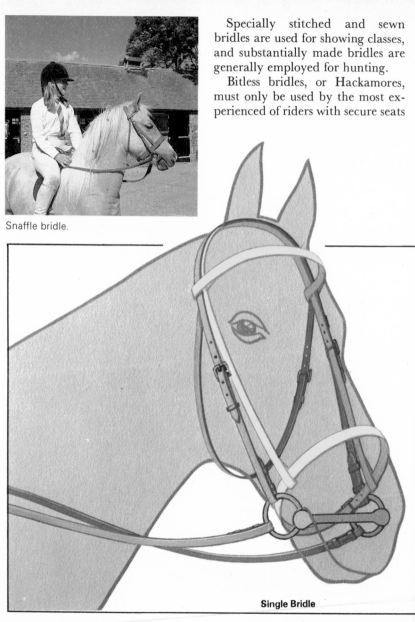

Snaffle bridle.

Single Bridle

and very light hands, for they are extremely severe.

Gag bridles consist of snaffles with hollow rings so that the reins are connected directly with the headpiece. They also are only for the experts.

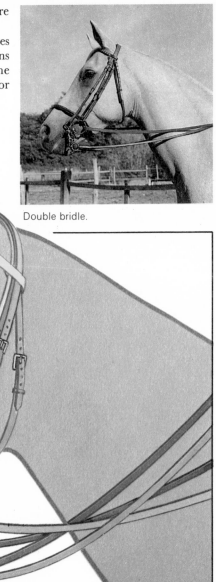

Double bridle.

Double Bridle

Fitting the bridle

A bridle must be fitted as carefully as a saddle, for an uncomfortable pony will never relax or be totally obedient to the aids. All the straps must be clean and supple and the bridle must be correctly assembled. With the bridle on the pony, the following points must be checked to see that it fits:–

Points to Check for a Well-fitting Bridle

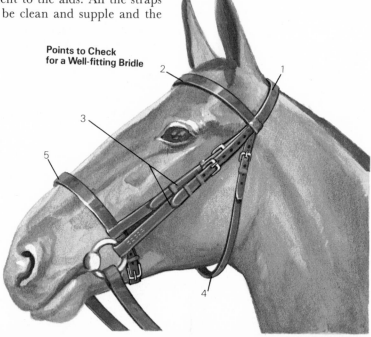

1   The headpiece must not rub the back of the ears.

2   The browband must not fit so tightly that it pulls the headpiece too far forward; on the other hand, neither should it hang too loosely downward.

3   The cheek pieces should hold the bit at the correct height.

4   The throatlatch should buckle up but there should be enough room to allow a clenched fist to be in-serted between it and the pony's throat.

5   You should be able to insert two fingers between the pony's nose and the noseband when it is fastened.

6   No buckles when fastened should press on any protruding bones of the pony's head.

7   No buckles should touch.

8   The general appearance of the bridle should be neat and comfort-able.

When buying a secondhand bridle, all the buckles should be undone and the straps should be carefully examined for signs of cracking. A neglected bridle will have cracks at the points where the leather passes through buckles and around the bit. Never use a bridle that is weakened in this way, the leather will give way under strain and you could have an accident.

Reins:

It is through the reins that the rider maintains contact with the pony's mouth. They must be kept supple and checked constantly for signs of wear, especially where they pass around the rings of the bit. There are many types of reins, and most snaffle bridles come complete with the medium-width plain leather rein, which buckles at the withers end. Some plain leather reins are very narrow and when wet, these are very difficult to grip. Plaited reins in which the leather is split and then plaited, give excellent grip, but do tend to stretch a little in use. Laced reins are very good in all situations; the leather is pierced and laced in a series of V-shapes which gives perfect grip even to wet or cold fingers. Rubber-covered reins are very good, but should be hand-sewn, and not machined, as this reduces their effectiveness in bad conditions. Nylon plaited reins become slimy and dangerous when wet, and then harsh and abrasive when dry. Plaited cotton Dartnall reins are excellent but expensive. They encourage a lightness of hand in the rider that cannot be achieved with any other reins.

Four types of reins, from left to right: plain leather, laced, Dartnall, plaited.

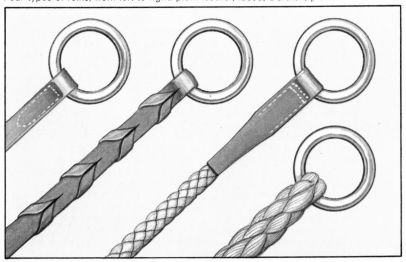

Snaffle bit too high – wrinkling the lips.

Bits

As we have said, the Snaffle is the standard bit. It is reasonably mild in its action and usually consists of two bit rings connected by a jointed mouthpiece. For the novice it is essential that the mouthpiece is fairly thick. A jointed snaffle acts rather like a nutcracker on the pony's jaw, and the thinner the mouthpiece, the more severe is the action. The German snaffle is par-

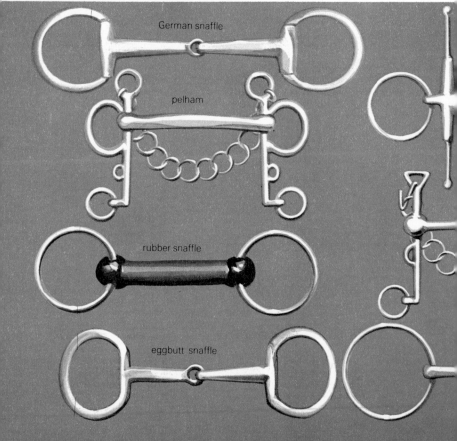

German snaffle

pelham

rubber snaffle

eggbutt snaffle

ticularly good; it has a thick but hollow mouthpiece, and is therefore very light in weight. In the Eggbutt snaffle the rings are fixed and cannot pinch the corners of the pony's lips.

The Racing snaffle is similar, but has 'dee' cheeks to prevent the bit being pulled through the animal's mouth. The mouthpiece is narrow, and the bit is more severe than the previous types.

The Twisted snaffle is a strong bit. It may have either eggbutt or loose

Snaffle bit too low – resting on the teeth.

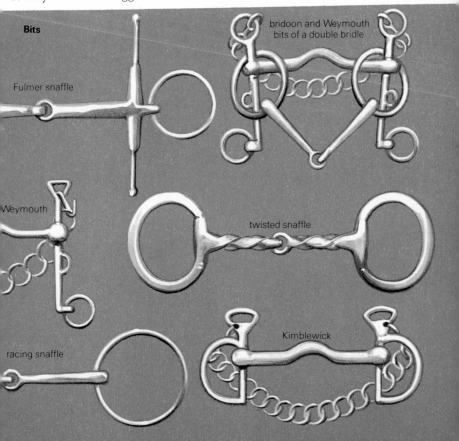

Bits

Fulmer snaffle

bridoon and Weymouth bits of a double bridle

Weymouth

twisted snaffle

racing snaffle

Kimblewick

rings, and the mouthpiece itself is twisted. It has a severe action and should only be used by an experienced rider on a pony with a very hard mouth.

There are many snaffle bits with straight, unjointed mouthpieces. The kindest are made of rubber or vulcanite, but these are often too mild for headstrong ponies.

For gymkhana events, spoon-cheek snaffles are useful, as the 'spoon' prevents the bit being pulled out of place in the excitement of the proceedings. These bits are also helpful in schooling young ponies, as the 'spoon' enables clear aids to be given with only a slight rein action. The Double Bridle has two bits, a bridoon or snaffle used in conjunction with a curb bit. Only experienced riders should use this type of bridle. For dressage the double bridle consists of an eggbutt bridoon and a Weymouth curb, complete with curb chain.

The Pelham is a variation of the curb, and attempts to combine the snaffle and curb in one bit. It is a useful bit for an excitable pony, and may be used with two reins, which is preferable, or the rings may be connected with roundings to which a single rein is attached. Many ponies go well in this bit. The Half-moon or Mullen Mouth Pelham is a

Running Martingale

popular bit. Its straight bar mouthpiece is comfortable even for a soft-mouthed pony.

The Eggbutt Pelham is similar and eliminates lip-pinching. The Rubber Mouth Pelham is a very mild bit, its main action being applied through the curb only. The Kimblewick is an excellent Pelham for jumping or hunting strong ponies usually ridden in snaffles. It is very short in the cheeks, and enables the rider to apply curb and poll pressure by keeping the hands low.

Martingales

Martingales are of three basic types and are used to prevent a pony throwing his head high to evade the action of the bit. The Standing martingale is the most simple and consists of a long strap with a loop at either end. The strap passes through a neckstrap to hold it in position, and one loop is fastened to the girth, having been passed between the forelegs. The other loop is attached to the noseband behind the pony's jaw. These martingales must not be adjusted too tightly, or the pony will loose all freedom of his neck muscles. It should be loose enough to allow a natural head carriage at all paces. Correctly fitted, the martingale will

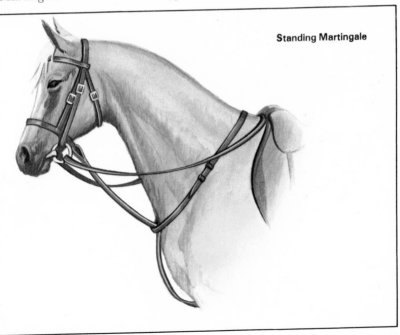

Standing Martingale

Martingales are artificial aids and very useful if fitted correctly and used intelligently. For hunting, they give added control when a horse or pony becomes over-excited.

not affect the pony's jumping abilities, as the head is not thrown up while jumping, but rather forward and down.

A Running martingale is the most popular for jumping competitions, its action is slightly more complex than that of the standing type. It consists of a strap from the girth, which passes between the forelegs and through a neckstrap, then divides into two pieces with a ring at either end. These rings, which should be small enough to prevent them catching over the bit rings or the bridle buckles, have the reins passed through them. This martingale achieves its effect through pressure on the pony's mouth. It is generally used with a snaffle bridle, or on the bridoon rein of a double bridle. The expert rider may use the martingale on the curb rein of a double bridle however, to make a dressage horse

Equipment for cleaning tack:
1 A firm support for the saddle – a saddle horse is best but two kitchen chairs can be used, placed back to back.
2 A strong hook for bridle, girth and leathers.
3 Dandy brush – to remove sweat from serge-lined saddles.
4 Bucket of warm water.
5 Rough cloth – for washing leatherwork.
6 Chamois leather.
7 Saddle soap.
8 Sponge.
9 Metal polish.
10 Leather dressing for oiling and preserving leather.
11 Smooth cloths – for applying metal polish and leather dressing.

flex the jaw. For safety, rubber stops should be used on the reins, towards the bit, to stop the martingale rings sliding forward.

An Irish martingale consists of a short piece of leather with a ring at either end through which the reins are passed. This very simple device is useful for a young or impetuous pony, as it stops the animal tossing his head about too much and prevents the reins from being thrown over the head. Stops on the reins should be used.

Martingales should be used intelligently. Many people add them to their tack list as a fashionable item, but no gadgetry should be used on any pony for its looks alone. Incorrectly fitted martingales can be positively dangerous.

Care of tack

Tack is expensive and must be kept soft, supple and clean in order to be safe in use. It should be cleaned every time it is used to maintain it in perfect condition. Hard, dirty

A saddle horse gives firm support.

tack is dangerous. It could break during use and cause a serious accident. Stiff, unyielding leather quickly rubs sore places on a pony's face; dirty saddles cause sore backs; and stiff girths produce nasty girth galls. A pony with any of these injuries must be rested and cannot be ridden, so tack cleaning time must be thought of as an important part of riding.

How to clean the saddle:

1 Put the saddle on its support.

2 Remove girth and stirrup leathers.

3 Holding the saddle on its pommel edge, brush the lining thoroughly with a dandy brush if it is lined with serge or linen. If it is leather-lined, use a rough cloth (towelling is ideal) and with the pommel edge over the bucket, remove every trace of dried sweat and mud.

4 With the saddle back on its support, wash every part with warm water, using a damp sponge, including those parts which are out of sight!

5 Dry the leather with the chamois.

6 Rinse the sponge, dampen it and use it to apply saddle soap over all the leatherwork. The soap should be well worked-in, and the underside of the flaps should receive extra attention. The girth straps are possibly the most important part of the saddle from a safety aspect, and these must be well cared for. The sponge must not be allowed to become too wet or the saddle soap will lather up and be less effective.

7 Hang stirrup leathers and leather girth on hook and wash well with a damp sponge before drying with the chamois leather. Other girths do not need washing every time they are used, but should be checked and brushed if necessary.

8 Apply saddle soap to leathers and leather girth, working it well in.

9 If the stirrup irons are muddy, wash them in the bucket, then dry

Cleaning the Saddle

1 The saddle is washed over all surfaces with warm water, including the underside.

2 All the leather is carefully cleaned with some saddle soap on a damp sponge.

them. Clean and polish the irons with metal polish and smooth lint-free cloths.

10 Reassemble the saddle and store neatly with the girth laid over the seat and the stirrups run up the leathers.

3 Work the soap well in, paying particular attention to the underside of the flaps.

4 The girth straps are possibly the most important part of the saddle from a safety aspect.

5 Wash leather girth and stirrup leathers well before drying with chamois leather.

6 If the stirrup irons are muddy, wash them, then dry and polish with metal polish.

How to clean the bridle:

1 Take the bridle to pieces and hang by the buckles from the hook.

2 Wash and dry the bit, ensuring that the mouthpiece, especially if jointed, is spotlessly clean.

3 Polish the rings (*not the mouth-piece*) with metal polish and soft cloths.

4 Wash the leather straps and buckles with the rough cloth.

5 Dry with the chamois leather.

6 Apply saddle soap to both sides of all the straps and work it well in.

7 Polish the buckles and make sure that they all work freely. A little vegetable oil may be applied to stiff buckles.

8 Reassemble bridle and hang it up neatly.

Cleaning other equipment:

All leatherwork can be cleaned in a similar fashion. It should be washed free of sweat and mud, dried, then soaped well. When the soap has dried, the leather can be polished with a leather dressing and a soft cloth – an old stable rubber or linen glasscloth is ideal. Buckles should be kept bright and clean.

Numnahs or saddle cloths can be regularly washed when necessary.

Cleaning the Bridle

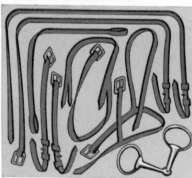

1 Take the bridle to pieces and then hang by the buckles from the hook.

2 Wash and dry the bit. Make sure the mouthpiece is very clean.

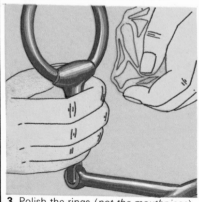

3 Polish the rings (*not the mouthpiece*) with metal polish and cloths.

4 Wash the leather straps and buckles.

Nylon and other washable girths must not be allowed to become stiff or they will cause serious galls. When washed, they must be thoroughly dried before use. Neglected or hard tack can be carefully oiled. The oil – there are several brands available – should be used mainly on the flesh, or underside, of the leather, where the pores are more open. The smooth or grain side has been waterproofed and will not absorb the oil to any great extent. Oil applied to the seat of the saddle can have a detrimental effect on your riding gear. Tack must not be over oiled or the leather becomes unpleasantly greasy.

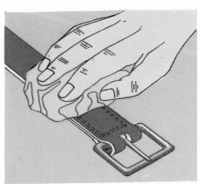

5 Dry thoroughly with the chamois leather.

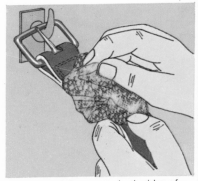

6 Apply saddle soap to both sides of all the straps and work it well in.

7 Polish buckles and make sure they work freely.

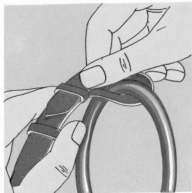

8 Reassemble bridle and hang it up neatly.

Tacking up

The saddle:

The saddle is put on from the near-side, when the pony is tied up. The stirrup leathers are attached and the irons 'run-up', and the girth is buckled to the offside girth straps.

Place the saddle high up on the withers, then slide it gently back to rest in the correct position. This ensures that all the hairs of the coat lie smooth and flat.

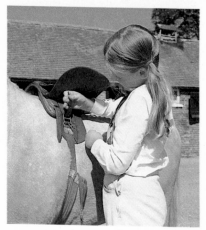

The girth is passed under the pony's belly, then all straps are securely fastened.

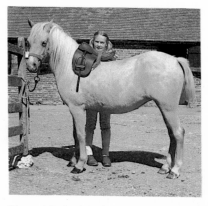

The saddle is placed on the withers and slid back into the correct position.

Pass to the offside of the pony and let the girth hang down, it should be about one hand's width behind the pony's elbow. Go back to the near-side and buckle up the girth. Care must be taken to ensure that the skin is smooth and that it is neither too tight nor too loose. Many ponies fill themselves with air when the girth is first buckled. It is always a good idea to buckle it fairly loosely at first, only tightening it before mounting. Checking the girth before mounting is a habit that should be acquired by all riders.

The stirrup irons may be pulled down to check the leathers are correctly adjusted.

The bridle:

To put on a bridle, the pony is approached from the nearside. The reins are passed over the head and the head collar rope is released. If the pony moves or is restless, he can be controlled by holding the reins. Nervous or naughty ponies can be restrained by having the head collar strapped lightly round the neck and tied up. Holding the bridle by the headpiece, the bit is taken in your left hand and pressed against the pony's teeth. If he does not open his mouth, your thumb can be used to

Next the cavesson noseband is buckled up and all strap ends put in their keepers.

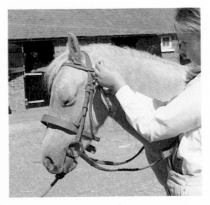

The bridle is put on from the nearside and the throat latch is fastened correctly.

encourage him to do so, by inserting it behind his front teeth. The bit slides into his mouth and the headpiece is slipped over his ears.

The bit should be fitted high enough to wrinkle the corners of the pony's mouth slightly: too high and the pony will resent the pain of it, too low and it will knock on his teeth.

The throatlatch is buckled and when fastened, there should be room for a clenched fist between the leather and the pony's throat.

The noseband should fit below the cheekbone, and when buckled, should allow for two fingers to be inserted between it and the pony's face.

A neat snaffle bridle with non-slip reins, presenting a smart appearance.

The Pony at Grass

A pony kept in a field at all times is said to be 'at grass' and has special requirements.

Fencing

Wooden post and rail is the best type of fencing for a pony's paddock. However it is very expensive to buy, erect and maintain. Properly prepared wooden posts are sunk into the ground and the rails are either nailed on or set into slots in the posts. Three rails are usually fixed, and the whole fence is regularly treated with preservative. When backed by a thick hedge, this ideal fencing looks good and also provides a fine windbreak.

An alternative to post and rails is to use wooden posts and three strands of tough wire. The posts must

Perhaps the safest, most permanent enclosure is a well-constructed brick or stone wall. Such walls are sometimes found on the divided sites of old country estates.

be erected every 3.5 metres (12 feet), or closer. Every fourth or fifth post should be extra tough and sunk well into the ground. The wire must be pulled very taut with a special gadget; the top strand should be about 105 centimetres (3.5 feet) from the ground, the bottom strand about 45 centimetres (1.5 feet) high and the centre strand stretched equally between these two.

Some ponies spend their time stretching across the top strand of a wire fence to get at the grass just out of reach. To stop this, it is possible to substitute barbed wire for the top strand of plain wire. Barbed wire must be used with caution as bad accidents can occur when it is allowed to sag and become loosened.

Sheep hurdles are not strong enough to keep ponies in their fields. Chestnut palings are sometimes used, but these are very dangerous indeed. They can break off, leaving jagged edges which cause injuries.

Most fields are already fenced or have old, thick hedges. Before put-

Natural hedgerows often need fortifying to prevent ponies escaping. Barbed wire is sometimes used but must be correctly stretched. Slack wire like this is dangerous.

ting a pony into a new field the perimeters must be thoroughly checked. Poke a thick stick into the hedge to check for any thin or weak spots. These must be properly reinforced by putting in two posts and wiring between. The hedge will soon grow thickly across, hiding the patch. Wooden fences should be checked for weaknesses and methodically repaired with new timber struts. All reinforcements should be nailed on from the inside of the field so that a pony leaning on them will put the strain against the posts or supports and not on the nails.

Electric fencing is only suitable for ponies when used within a properly fenced field, to enable it to be strip-grazed.

Gates

The weakest point of any field that is well fenced is bound to be the gate. Ponies can be very cunning and can

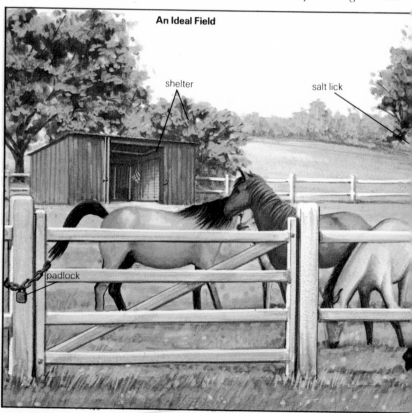

An Ideal Field

shelter

salt lick

padlock

learn to open many types of fastenings and bolts. They can push over temporary or makeshift gates, and a pony straying on the road is both a potential danger to other road users and in danger of being killed by traffic.

The best gates are properly constructed field gates of timber or metal. They are made so that they do not sag in use, but swing easily on well-oiled hinges – very important when you have an excited pony

post and rail fence

to hold with one hand, and the gate latch to contend with.

The gate needs to be as high as the fence and at least 1.2 metres (4 feet) wide. It should open into the field, not swing outwards. The hinges and latch should be well maintained, oiled often and kept rust-free. Self-locking catches do not always close properly and must be checked.

Cattle-proof catches are usually pony-proof too. If the pony's field is some distance away, it is a good idea to buy a length of chain to slip around the gate and the gatepost after it is firmly shut. A padlock with a coded combination can be used to secure the chain. Coded locks are better than those with keys, which can easily be lost. The code is set and should be easy to remember, such as a birthday or telephone number. When this number is dialled, the lock opens.

The gateway is a problem area in a field, especially in districts where the ground is of heavy clay. In wet weather the gateway can become a sea of mud. A load of hardcore, chalk, gravel or ash can be bought and tamped well into the ground in the gateway during the summer. It will more than repay its cost and effort during bad winter days.

If it is really impossible to buy a proper gate, a functional temporary one can be made from stout pieces of half round rail. The important thing is to have really firm, well set posts at either side of the gateway. Special D-shaped brackets can be screwed on to these and the ends of the rails slotted in. Old horse-shoes can be fixed to the posts instead of brackets and they are just as good.

Removable rail gateways have one drawback, you need two hands in order to take down the rails. When you are alone, it is not easy to cope with the rails and a pony simultaneously!

Grass

A good field will be full of lush green grass. The best grass for ponies is about 7–10 centimetres (3–4 inches) high, and does not contain too much clover. In Britain grass grows very little between October and March. It retains a fair amount of food value until the New Year, but after that provides only bulk. At the beginning of April, grass starts to grow in warmer areas. Through May, June and July, it reaches its peak of growth and has maximum food value. During August and September, it still grows, but the flavour diminishes and the food value declines.

It is very important to manage your grazing properly in order to get the best for your pony. One pony needs a minimum of 1 hectare (2.5 acres) and the area should be divided into two sections; this is the only time electric fencing may be used with ponies. Two sections are necessary so that one area can be rested and recover from grazing.

The most sheltered section should be used for the worst months of the winter, saving the other section for March or April. The winter plot will take 6 to 8 weeks to recover and get its spring growth of grass. Then the pony can be moved over once again. The winter area will recover even more quickly if a harrow and roller are run over it by a local farmer.

If the weather has been very wet, the pony will have churned up the ground, leaving deep hoofmarks in a sea of mud. This is known as 'poaching' the land, and such areas should be reseeded if possible. Heavy grazing takes a lot out of the land and it might be necessary to use some fertilizer. The pony must be kept off the field when the dressing is applied.

A pony will not eat grass soiled with its droppings, and large areas of the field can be wasted because of this. Droppings can be picked up at regular intervals, and the tall, rank grass which grows in these spots can be cut right down. Sometimes local gardeners can be found who are glad to collect the droppings from the field to use as fertiliser. All patches of coarse grass should be cut back to allow the finer, more succulent growths to come through.

Weeds

A pony grazing in a field full of glorious yellow dandelions, pink clover and tall purple thistles makes

Grazing is best managed by dividing into sections and using the areas in rotation.

a very pretty picture, but weeds take precious nourishment from the land; for too many weeds deprive the grass of minerals and cut down the food available to the pony. Weeds can be controlled quite easily with selective weedkillers, applied carefully while the pony is grazing the alternative plot. Weeds can also be pulled up by hand or cut back before they seed. Some plants are dangerous if the pony eats them and it is important to learn to recognise the poisonous ones.

The most common of these plants is the ragwort. It is easily overlooked before it flowers, but luckily few ponies will eat it at that stage of its development. Later, its abundant, bright yellow daisy-like flowers open, and this is when the plant can be cut out of the ground with a sharp spade. Ragwort is most lethal when it is withered or dried out in hay, so care must be taken to remove the plants from the field and, if possible, they should be burnt.

The beautiful common foxglove is

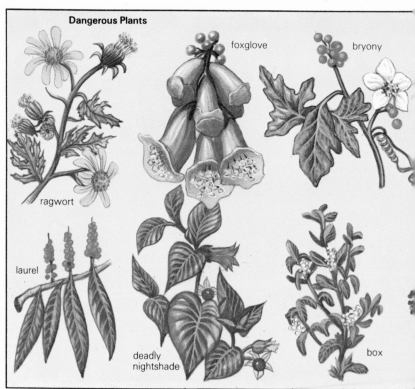

Dangerous Plants

foxglove

bryony

ragwort

laurel

deadly nightshade

box

equally dangerous to the pony, and should be pulled out if found growing in the pasture.

Deadly nightshade twines its way through shaded hedges and is highly toxic. Rhododendron, ivy and privet are also poisonous to ponies, and yew proves fatal in a very short time. Ponies rarely eat the first four shrubs unless clippings are tossed over the hedge for them, but they readily eat growing yew and green bracken, which is also dangerous.

Many plants are at their most toxic just as they wilt down and start to dry out. Other dangerous plants are lupins, laburnum, laurel and box. Even the seemingly innocuous grass clippings can be fatal to your pony. Sometimes well-meaning people feed such clippings, piling them in a neat heap on the ground. If the grazing is scanty, the pony may well devour the lot – with disastrous consequences. The clippings ferment within the pony's stomach and cause severe colic, which may be fatal. It is well worth a visit to any houses

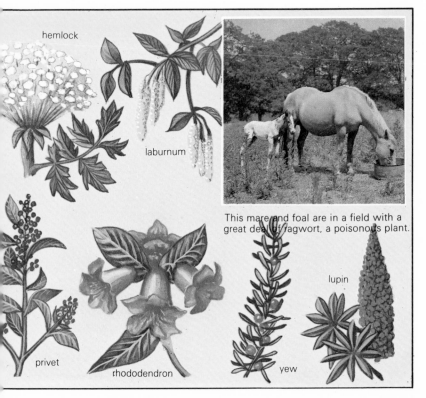

This mare and foal are in a field with a great deal of ragwort, a poisonous plant.

hemlock

laburnum

privet

rhododendron

yew

lupin

Suitable water containers should be easily cleaned and safe like the two at the top. Old baths and buckets can be dangerous in use.

adjacent to the pony's field to explain the dangers of feeding *anything* to the pony other than its normal diet. (For emergency treatment in cases of poisoning see the section on First Aid, page 152).

Water

One of the most important things about your pony's field is that it should have a suitable water supply. There is nothing so time-consuming and unpleasant as carrying buckets of water to the field in winter. The very best way of supplying water is to have a self-regulating tank piped in to the main water supply. This is operated by a ballcock which should be checked daily, for if this gets clogged up with debris, the system breaks down.

Few fields have facilities for such a water supply however, and the next best thing is to have a length of reinforced hosepipe running from the galvanised tank in the field to any convenient tap. The hose should be left in place: it can be buried or run along the hedgerow, but it must be very well lagged for use in winter. It is important that the pony cannot play with the hose or trample on it. Never leave the end of the hose in the tank after filling it – when the other end is removed from the tap all the water may be siphoned out again.

A proper galvanised tank or large pan is the only sensible way to hold the pony's water. Buckets do not hold enough and get knocked over, kicked and buckled. Old bath tubs look dreadful and the rims can be dangerous. Plastic tubs and bins are too fragile to last long.

The tank must not be too tall, or too big. Too tall and the pony will not be able to drink comfortably; too big and you will not be able to tip the water out in order to give the tank its regular clean.

The tank should be scrubbed out with a stiff brush and clean water every 3 months. Do not use detergent. Any stubborn algae stains can be removed with a weak solution of household bleach in a bucket of cold water. Rinse around with clear water afterwards and refill. Make sure the tank does not get filled with falling leaves in the autumn. As these decay they may release toxins into the water. And do not site the tank under a tree where birds roost. The droppings of some birds can cause disease in other animals.

Shelter

Most ponies can live quite happily out at grass all year round if they are well fed, have a good winter coat and can shelter from the winter winds. A really good hedge acts as a perfect windbreak if sited on the north side of the field. Windbreaks can be made from sheep hurdles and straw bales, carefully erected. These should be in a zigzag or box formation partly for strength, and partly to afford protection at different angles as the prevailing winds shift and veer. The hurdles are of close woven split stakes made with long wooden spikes to knock into the ground. The edges of the hurdles should be securely lashed or wired together. For even more protection, straw bales can be piled behind the hurdles, but these should be covered with polythene sheeting and wired off securely to the adjoining fence to stop the pony pulling them to pieces.

A wooden field shelter is excellent if properly constructed and sited. A bad shelter can do more harm than good. A wet or damp pony confined in a draughty shelter will quickly chill and may become seriously ill. For a single pony, an ideal shelter would be about 3.5 × 3 metres (12 × 10 feet). For two ponies, a shelter of 4.5 × 3.5 metres (14 × 12 feet) is about right. The floor is very important and can be of tamped chalk or concrete, laid to a slight slope on a hardcore base. The floor must extend well outside the open side of the field shelter to prevent the interior getting filled with mud. The open side of the shelter should have two long poles fitted into metal brackets to act as a gate when necessary.

The object of a field shelter is to allow the pony to escape from the very worst weather. A pony should never be tied up or confined in a three-sided building for any length of time or he will become chilled.

The pony should be allowed to

use the shelter and to go in and out as and when he wishes. Cold will never harm a well-fed pony which is able to exercise freely. A good field shelter provides respite from continuous rain in winter and from the irritation of biting flies in summer. It must be kept fresh and clean, and the droppings picked up regularly. Food and water containers should be washed frequently, and an impregnated fly strip can be hung from the roof in early summer.

Summer routine

In summer, the grass grows thick and rich, and the pony will eat around the clock if allowed to do so. If restricted to about 0.5 hectare (an acre) of land the pony will probably stay reasonably slim, especially if ridden every day. If he is turned out on a larger plot however, it would be better to confine him to the field shelter or a stable during the main part of the day. This not only pro-

A Good Shelter

Whether or not he is being ridden, the pony at grass must be checked every day. This pony has lost condition and become overweight, so he could succumb to laminitis.

tects the pony from biting insects, but also prevents him becoming overweight.

The pony should be visited every day, even when he is not to be ridden. The water must be checked, making sure there is an ample supply and that it is fresh and clean. In summer, people have a habit of tossing all kinds of junk into fields – paper bags, bottles and cans – and it is wise to check the ground regularly. If a bottle is trodden on and broken the jagged edges may seriously cut the pony's pasterns.

Flies can be a great nuisance to the grass-fed pony, settling in clusters around the eyes and nostrils. Some flies lay their eggs on the pony's coat, others actually under the skin, and these cause swellings and irritation. If he rubs his head to get rid of flies, the pony may get abrasions on the bony areas of the face. These should be treated with an antiseptic, fly-repelling cream to heal and protect the wounds. Special fly repellent lotions can be bought and sponged on to the pony's coat. Applied correctly and at the proper intervals, these products make the pony's life much happier during the midsummer months.

Specially fringed browbands can be attached to the head collar. As the pony moves his head while grazing, the fringes continuously brush away the flies and other biting insects. Two ponies living together will stand head to tail, side by side, each swishing the flies from the other's face with his tail.

If the pony is ridden a great deal

Flies are troublesome in summer but fringed browbands are available.

during the summer holidays, a little supplementary feeding in the form of pony cubes should be given at least one hour before riding. Special care must be taken when riding out in summer. There are many vehicles which may be strange to the pony, such as tractors with various attachments, or cars pulling caravans. The inviting grassy verges may conceal drains and gullies which could bring the pony down. You should never ride through thick undergrowth along unknown paths in case of unseen hazards.

Laminitis

One unpleasant result of over-grazing by the pony is the condition known as *laminitis*. Not all ponies succumb to this, even though they might be allowed to get grossly fat, but some are subject to the painful disease after only a few days of gorging on lush spring grass.

Laminitis is the inflammation of the laminae, the fleshy tissues inside the pony's foot. Because the hoof is solid, the swollen parts press against the inside wall and the pony experiences severe pain. One, or all of the feet may be affected, and the pony is loath to put any weight on the painful area.

The forefeet are most commonly affected, but when a pony has laminitis in all four feet he is a pitiful sight. He tries to relieve the weight by adopting a typical stance, with all four feet held as far forward as

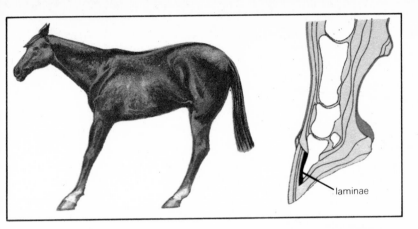

laminae

Laminitis, the inflammation of the laminae, is one unpleasant result of over-grazing.

possible trying to get some of the weight on to the heels. Quite often the pony seeks relief by lying down flat on his side, all four legs extended; then he is reluctant to get up again.

Laminitis can be caused in ponies by excessive overwork, or conversely by long periods of enforced idleness in confined quarters. The most common cause however, is too much new and very rich grass. Ponies will eat such succulent growth without pause, if given the chance. And if they are prone to laminitis, a severe attack will soon follow.

Such vulnerable ponies must be kept away from the grass during the daytime, and allowed to graze only at night. They must be exercised carefully and thoroughly every day and watched for the first signs and symptoms of pain.

If your pony gets an attack of this painful disease, the veterinary surgeon must be called. He can give injections which reduce the flow of blood to the feet, and help to reduce the pressure and pain. You can place the affected feet in buckets of cold water, then add ice cubes to reduce the temperature of the water. The blacksmith can help by fitting special shoes to relieve the pain on the soles, but as in so many things connected with ponies and riding, prevention is better than cure.

Catching up

If a pony is difficult to catch he should be turned out wearing a head collar. It is very important, however, that this fits well and is properly made. A good head collar should be adjustable, and have very secure, good quality buckles. It should preferably be made of leather, but some of the cheaper nylon ones are satisfactory if of a reputable brand. If a head collar does not fit

Head collars should be kept clean and must be fitted correctly to prevent chafing.

something to grab when the pony is near. Sometimes, sitting or kneeling on the ground works – the pony is overcome with curiosity and comes to see what you are doing. A bucket with a small feed should be given after the pony is safely in hand. Never chase a difficult pony, he just gets more and more excited. Get close up to him, then let him take the last few steps towards you for his reward.

The pony with a head collar is led by affixing a rope with a spring clip to the ring behind the chin. The head collar must be kept clean and supple, and in long periods of wet weather the nylon type must be removed or it will rub large patches of hair off the pony's face.

Turning out

When turning the pony out after riding, first make absolutely certain that he is cool, and not still sweating. If he is, you must lead him quietly around until every part is cool and dry. The places to check are under the elbow and behind the ears.

Take the pony into the field, turn him round and close the gate. Stand near the gate with the pony's head towards you and remove the rope, halter or head collar, then give a favourite titbit. Never encourage the pony to gallop away; this is dangerous and you might be kicked. Turn decisively away and go through the gate, shutting it carefully behind you.

well it can come off, or, much worse, the pony can catch his foot in the straps while grazing or scratching.

When catching your pony, you can teach him to come when you call. It is very frustrating indeed to have a pony you find difficult to catch, and it is sensible to catch him quite often, just for a pat and a reward, and not only when you wish to go riding. Ponies are cunning creatures and can soon associate being caught with having to do some strenuous exercise. If the pony is easy to catch, the head collar or halter can be slipped on in the field, then the pony is given a reward – a few cubes or some sliced apple or carrot, and petted.

A pony that is habitually difficult to catch must be taught that good things only happen after he has behaved well. A short piece of rope attached to the head collar gives you

Care in Winter

A well-fed pony will not normally suffer from the cold conditions of winter, especially if he has a sheltered field. Most ponies, unless highly bred, will grow thick, natural winter coats which give perfect protection against the elements. If a pony lives out in winter he should not be groomed very much or the natural grease in his coat which helps to keep him warm will be removed. However, a pony which is required to undertake strenuous work during the winter months and also lives out may be trace clipped to prevent undue sweating. If this is done, the pony should be provided with a New Zealand rug to wear in the field. In trace clipping, the hair is removed from the pony's belly, the girth region, between the forelegs and the underside of the neck. It must be carried out with proper clippers and by an expert. This form of clipping enables the pony to hunt and jump without the excessive sweating that occurs if his thick winter coat covers these areas.

A pony in winter, trace clipped and provided with a rug, can have the rest of the coat cleaned and groomed thoroughly before the rug is fitted. New Zealand rugs are made of canvas or nylon material. They are proof against wind and rain, and are warmly lined with woollen or quilted nylon material. Perhaps the most important thing about a New Zealand rug is that it must fit the pony perfectly. A badly-fitting rug

In autumn, ponies at grass grow thick coats which help protect them from cold.

Thin-coated horses and ponies may be turned out in New Zealand canvas rugs.

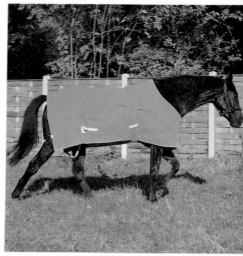

or one with incorrectly fastened straps will come loose or slip while the pony is turned out, with possibly fatal consequences.

Whatever the weather, the rug must be taken off and its lining be brushed every day. The pony's coat is also brushed smooth and clean at this time. All the straps of the rug must be kept clean and supple, and all the areas where these may rub the skin must be inspected. The rug must not be used if the pony is brought in; since it is waterproof, sweat cannot evaporate through the fabric, and the rug acts like a sweat suit in warm conditions. For this reason also, the rug must never be put on to a pony that is hot or sweating.

Ponies turned out with a full winter coat will regularly roll in the deepest, wettest mud that they can find. Although this makes life tough for their owners who have to remove the mud before riding out, it does serve as a natural protection against the cold. There is nothing you can do to prevent mud rolling by the pony kept at grass, and the pony's welfare is more important than a little extra work in grooming.

During the winter months it is vital to stick to a firm routine in caring for the pony at grass. He expects to be fed at the same time each day, and when the mornings and evenings are dark, there can be problems. The pony must be visited, if not ridden, at least twice daily in the winter – to feed him and some-

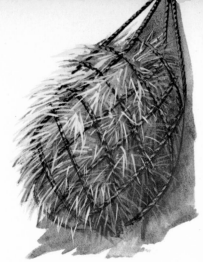

Using a haynet is the only sensible way to feed hay to your pony.

times to break the ice on the water tank. When feeding hay it is convenient to have two haynets; one can be filled and taken to the field, then the empty one is brought back and filled ready for the next feed. Using a haynet is the only sensible way to feed hay to your pony. If hay is put on the ground it gets trampled on and wasted.

A haynet, tied-up with a proper knot at the correct height for your pony, allows him to eat without wasting any, and it aids digestion. If you have a shelter, always feed the pony inside it. This will encourage the pony to use the shelter and the haynet will keep dry in wet weather. If the pony is in hard work such as hunting, extra food must be given. Specially formulated cubes are the most convenient to store, measure out, and feed without waste.

Ponies often roll in mud which clings to the thick coat forming a protective layer.

then used to cover the bucket, and it is left to cool. Making a perfect bran mash is quite difficult, but practice enables you to judge exactly the right amount of water. When properly made, the finished mash is crumble-dry, not too stiff and sticky, not wet and porridge-like. It can be fed when it feels comfortably warm if you plunge your hand to the bottom of the bucket. Ponies love sweet things, and a little treacle, molasses or brown sugar can be added as a treat.

Linseed is sometimes given to ponies in the winter months. It improves the condition and appearance of the coat. Linseed is very expensive, but only a little is fed at a time. About 0.25 kilogram ($\frac{1}{2}$lb) of linseed is put into a large saucepan, covered with cold water and left to soak overnight. Next day it is rinsed, covered with fresh water and brought to the boil. After simmering

Most ponies appreciate a hot bran mash now and again after work. This is made by filling a bucket about two-thirds full with good quality broad bran. Pour a little boiling water evenly over the bran and stir until it is all just wetted. A tea-towel is

Riding in winter

A pony out at grass in the winter must be carefully warmed up before being strenuously exercised, for he is unlikely to be very fit. There are rules for winter riding:

1 Always walk your pony for at least the first 10 minutes of a ride.
2 Keep a steady pace on an unfit pony – no racing or galloping about, just steady trotting and perhaps one gentle canter.
3 Always walk your pony home

for the last 15 or 20 minutes of the ride. Loosen the girth a little.
4 Always get home before dark.
5 At home undo the girth and bridle straps and run the stirrups up their leathers. If the pony is still warm, lead him around, with the saddle still in place, until he has cooled off.
6 Offer a small bucket of water to which a cupful of boiling water has been added to take the chill off.
7 Turn the pony out to roll.
8 Feed in the field or shelter.

for a few moments it is removed from the heat and allowed to cool, when it forms a jelly which can be mixed with the normal feed. Linseed jelly must be fed daily over a period of at least two weeks before its effect can be seen.

Hunting:

If a pony is to be hunted in winter it must first be conditioned. This is the term used for converting an animal in soft, unfit condition into one that is sound and fit and ready to go.

The first thing in conditioning is to have the blacksmith shoe the pony suitably for heavy work. Then a week of gradually increased walking exercise is undertaken, 20–30 minutes the first day, building up to an hour or more. At this stage the pony's saddle region and head must be checked for any signs of soreness. During the next week, extra hard feed is given, and the pony is trotted slowly for long periods combined with the walking.

At first the pony will sweat profusely and lather along the neck, but by the end of the second week, this will diminish significantly and the pony's rounded stomach will change shape as the muscles tone up. During the third and fourth weeks the walking and trotting continues. The first and last 20 minutes are spent walking briskly, well up to the bridle, not just strolling along. Some of the trotting should be up hills. The exercise period is increased and varied if possible: two sessions some days, if the weather is fine. Hound-jogging, which is a slow, even and steady trot, is the perfect pace for getting a pony fit. It does wonders for humans too! In the fifth and sixth weeks the pony has his hard feed stepped up yet again. The exercising is much as before, with the occasional canter

Mounted and foot followers move off from the meet for a day out with the foxhounds.

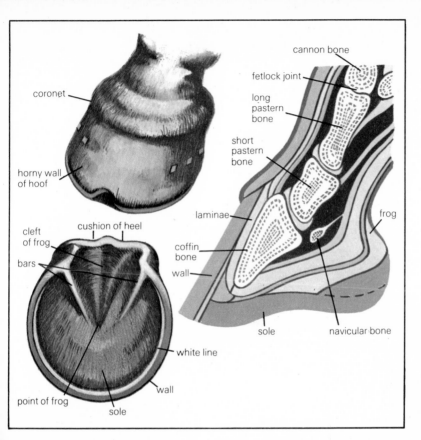

added for variety, but galloping and jumping are kept for the hunting field. Six weeks of this methodical exercising gets the pony fit.

Shoeing and the pony's feet

Care of the feet:

The most important aspect of pony care is looking after the animal's feet. The old maxim 'no foot, no horse' is repeated in practically every book on the care of ponies and horses. This is as it should be, for of all the old sayings it is the one that is most important and true. The pony's foot is made up of layers of horn which are insensitive and growing continuously, just like our fingernails. Within this tough outer wall are the soft laminae, fleshy leaves which are sensitive to pain. It is these that become inflamed in laminitis

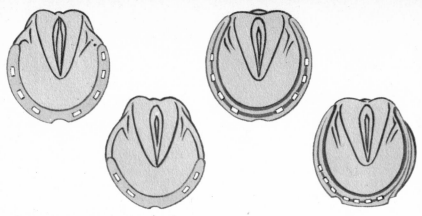

Types of shoes, from left to right: half-shoe, tip, seated-cut and fullered shoe.

(see page 108). The soft laminae surround the bones of the foot. When looked at from beneath, the visible part of the foot is the horny sole, which protects the inner sensitive sole. The large, firm, wedge-shaped structure coming in from the heel is the frog, and it should touch the ground in a correctly shod pony. Its function, apart from weight-bearing, is to act as a shock-absorber and anti-slip device.

Some ponies have such hard feet that they never need shoeing (see Caspian pony, page 60), others only require shoes on the forefeet which take extra wear.

A few ponies have feet of such soft horn that they wear down very quickly. Such ponies must be carefully shod in the first instance and watched carefully for signs of wear on the shoes, when these must be replaced without delay. When ponies live wild, the horn wears down naturally and the feet grow open, round and healthy. Domesticated ponies must have the regular attentions of the blacksmith and, even if ridden unshod, the feet still need to be trimmed and checked by him. Overlong, neglected feet soon develop cracks and splits in the horn. These may spread upwards and cause the pony to go lame for many weeks.

A pony out at grass should always have his feet inspected before being ridden out. The pony is tied up, and a hoofpick is used to remove any mud and stones from inside the foot and around the frog. The outside of the hoof, as well as the fetlock and pastern, should be brushed clean and the heels checked for any signs of cracking or sponginess. Either condition should be taken care of by drying the heels carefully and applying an ointment provided by the veterinary surgeon. Keeping the heels dry will prevent them from cracking.

If the foot smells rather peculiar, it could be due to an unpleasant condition of the frog, known as *thrush*, which must receive attention.

Shoeing:

There are two methods of shoeing a pony; one is hot shoeing, which is the traditional way. The farrier makes a shoe for each of the pony's feet, shaping each one in the fire of the forge, and working it with a hammer on the anvil until it fits perfectly.

Cold shoeing is the term for using ready-made shoes which are selected to fit the pony's feet as well as possible.

It does not need a lot of thought to appreciate that hot shoeing is by far the finest method. Sometimes the local farrier has a forge near enough for your pony to be taken for attention every two months or so.

Some farriers have portable forges and bring all their equipment to you, on a regular basis. This is sometimes easier to arrange if a group of friends with ponies fix joint 'farrier days' at one venue.

Blacksmith's Tools

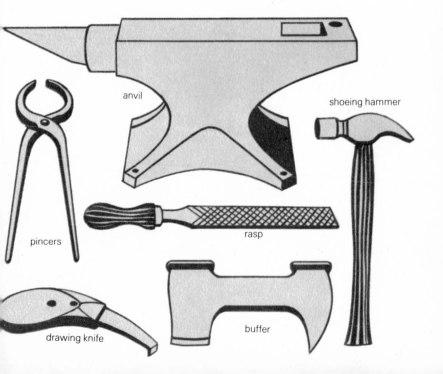

anvil

shoeing hammer

pincers

rasp

drawing knife

buffer

Hot shoeing:

Removal – the first thing the farrier does is to remove the old shoes. He cuts the clenches (see below) using the buffer and the driving hammer before levering off the shoe with the pinchers.

Preparation – next the foot is prepared for receiving the new shoe.

The sole and frog are cleaned-out and thoroughly checked, and the shape of the foot is adjusted by re- moving the overgrowth of horn with the drawing knife. Grossly long horn will be taken off with a special horn cutter. Very ragged parts of the sole or frog may be trimmed off, but basically these structures are left alone. The rasp is then used to make the bottom of the foot level.

Forging – this is the making of the new shoe, and here the craftsman really comes into his own, selecting the correct weight and type of iron

Hot Shoeing

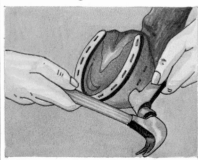
1 Cutting the clenches in order to remove the old shoe.

2 The sole and frog are cleaned, and thoroughly checked.

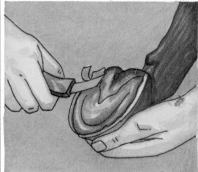
3 Removing the overgrowth of horn with the drawing knife.

4 Rasping the foot to make the bottom level.

and fashioning the entire shoes complete with clips and nail holes. The hot shoe may be tried against the prepared foot several times before the smith is satisfied. The application of the red-hot iron to the hoof marks the horn and indicates the fine adjustments to be made in the fit. Only when it aligns perfectly with the foot does the farrier plunge the hot iron shoe into cold water to cool and temper it.

Nailing on – special nails are used to attach the shoes to each foot, and they must be positioned with great accuracy through the insensitive part of the wall.

The ends of the nails are then twisted off, and the ends are rasped down and hammered flat. These are called the clenches. To finish off, the farrier taps the toe lightly home and runs the rasp lightly round the join between hoof and shoe.

5 Applying the red-hot iron to the hoof marks the horn.

6 The hot shoe is plunged in cold water to cool and temper it.

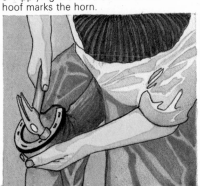

7 Nailing the shoe on. The nails must be positioned with great accuracy.

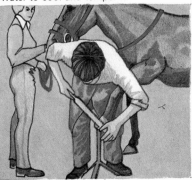

8 The farrier taps the shoe lightly and runs the rasp around the join.

A farrier at work, using the 'hot shoeing' method.

Worming and disease prevention

Worms:
While all ponies harbour worms, those kept at grass are particularly at risk of re-infection, and so need extra special attention. A small field used for grazing ponies over a number of years is probably horse-sick, and has many more worms than a field which has been rested,

or used to graze cattle. If the pony is generally healthy, his normal infestation of worms will not bother him unduly, but when any minor illness attacks the pony, the added worm burden may make him a very sick animal indeed. It is only commonsense therefore, to give all ponies regular doses of worming medicines.

Many preparations are effective against a wide range of these parasites, but if after worming consistently the pony still has an open, dull coat, and is generally listless, it is advisable to take a fresh sample of its dung to the veterinary surgeon. Examination under the microscope will soon indicate just which type of worm is infecting the pony and a special dose of vermicide can be made up. To give worming powders, keep the pony in his shelter, or tied up in the shade until he is really hungry, then make up a small feed of his favourite treats – bran, oats or maize. Mix the worm powder thoroughly into this and sprinkle brown sugar all over the top. Most ponies eat the preparation without any trouble. If a pony is difficult to fool in this way, the worm medicine can be given in syrup or liquid form with a long syringe.

Tetanus:

The only other regular disease prevention measure that is essential for any pony is a yearly injection against tetanus or lockjaw. Tetanus germs live in the soil and gain access to the body through a cut or abrasion.

A thin pony with ribs showing as a result of poor grazing and a worm burden.

The dreadful disease develops about ten days later and is usually fatal. It is a simple and vital matter to have your pony protected against tetanus. There is a serum which can be injected within 24 hours of the pony being cut or injured; but better than this there is a special Tetanus Toxoid, which is given as a precautionary measure and boosted every year by injection. Every pony should have protection against tetanus, and those who work with animals and may receive cuts or abrasions should also consider discussing with their doctor the possibility of protection for themselves against this terrible disease.

The Stabled Pony

The loose box is the best type of stable for a pony. It allows freedom and comfort, and the pony can get down to rest whenever he wishes. The box should be about 3 × 3 metres (10 × 10 feet) for a small pony, while a large horse would require one at least 4.5 × 3.5 metres (14 × 12 feet). The loose box door should be 1.2 metres (4 feet) wide for safety and must open outwards. An inward opening door disturbs the bedding, and it would be impossible to get into the box if, for instance, the pony became cast (unable to get up) near the door.

Correctly designed latches should be fitted to the door of the loose box,

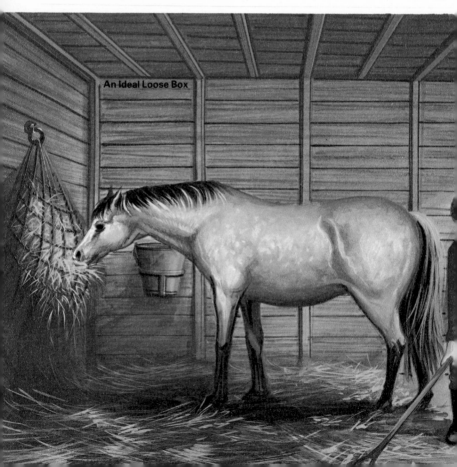

An Ideal Loose Box

one at the top of the lower door and another at the bottom to act as an anti-kicking bolt. Some ponies kick at the lower door when they are waiting for their food, and this can soon weaken the structure. Another single bolt is fixed to the upper door to close it at night or during bad weather. Hooks are attached to the doors to enable them to be fixed in an open position when required.

Most loose boxes are made of

A loose box prevents boredom because the pony can look over the lower door.

timber boards on a robust framework. Some are built of brick or block construction. It is important that the box has an impervious floor. The very best stables have brick floors, but concrete is a cheaper alternative. It must be properly laid so that it slopes slightly to allow for drainage, and should have a non-slip finish.

The loose box must have good ventilation to prevent the pony getting a stable cough. There should be a window with a top opening that opens inwards. All the glass must be covered with some form of mesh or bars to protect it from being broken by the pony.

Inside the loose box a few fittings are required. They should be properly designed and without any sharp edges which could damage the pony. A ring, fitted at chest-level, is necessary for tying the pony at the manger while the box is cleaned. Another, at eye-level, is useful for tying the pony up short while it is being groomed. This is known as short-racking. A high ring is provided for tying up the haynet if used. The rings must be securely fitted, preferably bolted right through one of the timber frames of the box. Hay may be fed in a fitted metal rack, but this must not be so high that hay seeds or dust fall in the pony's eyes.

Metal bucket holders are excellent when fitted at chest-level. They hold the bucket securely and prevent damage and waste. It two are fitted they can be used for food and water.

Bedding

Wheat straw makes the best bedding material but when it is in

Bedding must be carefully spread, shaking the straw well to break up any clumps. The straw is then laid in a thick, even layer over the floor and raised higher round the walls.

short supply, wood shavings from a reliable source or even shredded paper can be used. Soiled straw bedding has value as manure. Soiled shavings or paper have none. Oat straw is often advertised as bedding, but you may find your pony eats it!

Making a straw bed:

The bale of straw is taken into the box, and the twine cut and carefully disposed of – it is dangerous to leave strings of any kind in a stable. Next, the straw must be shaken well to separate it, using a long-pronged fork. Spread the straw thickly in the box. The bed should be deep and comfortable and the straw spread a little higher around the walls as a protection against draughts or possible injury.

Making a bed of shavings:

Shavings can be used alone or mixed with sawdust. It is possible to buy both, ready baled, from woodyards. They should be bought only from a clean, busy and efficient works to ensure that they are not contaminated by the droppings of rats and other vermin. This bedding must be spread thickly after the bales are opened, and the very tightly compressed material separated and loosened. Shredded paper is also purchased in tightly compressed bales, and spread in a very thick bed. It is a very cheap form of bedding for the pony.

Making a bed of peat moss:

Another material which can be used in the loosebox is peat moss. It makes a soft and comfortable bed and can be used as deep litter. This means that a very deep initial bed is laid in the box at the beginning of winter and only the very wet portions and, of course, the droppings are removed each day. A little fresh peat is added to the box daily, and the rest of the bed is left undisturbed. The whole box is cleaned out thoroughly in the spring. A deep litter bed can only be made in a box with excellent drainage, or it will soon become smelly and unhealthy for the pony. A properly made and maintained deep litter box can provide peat suitable for spreading on the surface of a schooling ring, or any parts of the field which are inclined to be 'poached' in winter (see page 100).

The stable – mucking out

In order to keep the stable fresh and wholesome it must be mucked out properly, unless the deep litter system is being used. To muck out straw bedding the following equipment is used:

1 a stable barrow,
2 a stable shovel,
3 a broom with stiff bristles,
4 a stable fork with blunt tines,
5 a four-pronged fork,
6 a skep or plastic laundry basket,
7 a plastic sheet or one made of a split hessian sack.

First thing in the morning, the pony is removed from the box or short-racked with a small feed while the clean straw is separated from the droppings with the stable fork. The clean straw is heaped around the side of the box, while the soiled bedding is forked into the stable barrow.

Barely soiled straw is retained and spread loosely on the fresh straw at the sides of the box, using the four-pronged fork. When the centre of the floor is clear, it is thoroughly brushed and any small debris is shovelled up and also put in the barrow. The straw can be left to dry, and the floor to air during the morn-

In this attractive old stable yard, the range of loose boxes has a thatched roof which provides extra warmth in winter and keeps the interiors cool during the summer months.

When mucking out, the clean straw is separated from the soiled using a special fork, then the muck is removed and placed in a wheelbarrow ready to take to the muck-heap.

ing. The pony is untied, and the barrow wheeled to the manure heap.

At midday, the bedding should be spread so that the pony can rest in the afternoon. Any droppings are picked up in the skep, then the lightly soiled straw is spread in the centre of the floor with clean straw on top. Fresh straw is added, to make the bed to the required thickness, and well-tossed.

During the rest of the day, droppings and wet straw must be removed and the bedding is tossed up once again at night. If necessary, a little more clean straw may be added. Straw should be carried in a hessian or heavy plastic sheet from storage shed to stable to prevent pieces spilling and blowing around, giving an unsightly apperance. Loose straw should be swept up from outside the stable door and put on the manure heap.

To make a manure heap, the soiled straw is first placed to make a small rectangle – 2.5 × 1.2 metres (8 × 4 feet) is a convenient size if you have one pony. The walls are built about 1 metre (3 feet) high, then the centre is filled in. By walking on the surface each day, and spreading the muck evenly, a neat and well compacted heap can be formed. When it is too high for you to reach easily, start a new heap. Keep the sides clean and square by teasing out loose straw with a fork. After a few months the heap shrinks down and after nine months the manure can be used by gardeners.

When using shavings or sawdust, a similar procedure is followed, except that the absorbent material soaks up the urine very readily and the whole wet patch can be taken up with a shovel. Droppings can be taken up from shavings very easily, using a household dustpan and brush.

Feeding

A stabled pony must be fed at regular intervals throughout the day. The amount of each feed depends upon the size of the pony and the nature of his work. Every horse and pony owner has ideas about the perfect feeding formula, but possibly the most convenient and least wasteful method for feeding is to use special cubes. Some cubes are made to supplement a hay diet, and some are made to substitute the hay as well. When buying a new pony it is as well to check on his usual diet and to stick to this until he has had time to settle in his new home. After two or three weeks, the constitutents of the diet can be changed gradually until he's eating the food you choose.

Types of food:

Hay is nutritious and provides essential bulk. Farmers make hay in June and July and it can often be bought 'off the field'. This means it is literally bought as it is being made and will be delivered to your home, rather than being stored in the farmer's barn, and consequently it is much cheaper.

Hay must be stored for at least six months before it is fed to your pony. Careful calculation will enable you to judge how much to buy to ensure you always have a supply ready for the pony to eat. Good hay is a pale green/gold colour, and smells wholesome and sweet. Bad hay has a musty smell. It is dull brown in colour and may contain weeds. Dark brown patches in the hay indicate that it was not dried properly before baling, or that the bales were soaked with rain on the field. It is pointless to try to feed bad hay to your pony. Even if the pony eats it, there will be little nourishment in the feed and some weeds may actually do harm.

Hay is best fed from a rack or haynet to prevent waste. The net is filled with the required weight of hay, then tied at head height to a convenient ring in the stable.

Straw can be fed as a substitute for half of the normal hay feed in years when the hay crop has failed, and any available hay is very expensive. Straw for feeding must be of good quality, smelling sweetly clean and of a dark golden colour. Oat straw is most acceptable, and barley straw can be used if free from the irritating awns (the spiky bits). Hard food is the name given to manufactured cubes, oats and other grains, bran and sugar beet.

Cubes enable the pony to receive a properly balanced ration without your having to weigh and measure several different foodstuffs. They are formulated for all types of horse and pony, and for animals in soft or hard work. It is sensible to buy the correct cubes and to measure them out accurately. They are highly concentrated and therefore weigh heavily. Cubes are made from a variety of ingredients depending on their formula, and include such things as oats, bran, barley, maize, beans, linseed, groundnuts, grass-meal and molasses, as well as the added minerals and vitamins necessary for the pony's good health and well-being.

Ponies on cubes work well without hotting up as they are apt to do on a diet of oats. Cubes are fairly expensive, however, and have a very low moisture content. Fresh water must be readily available to ponies

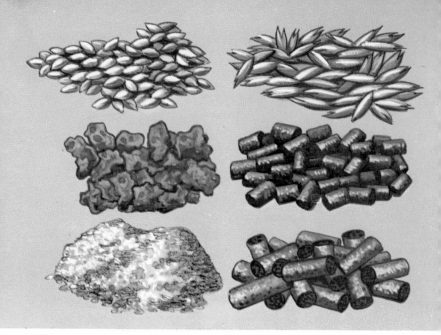

Different sorts of 'hard' food: top, left: barley; right: oats. Centre, left: maize; right: sugar beet pulp cubes. Bottom, left: bran; right: cubes.

fed on cubes, and a little bran added to the feed aids digestion.

Oats are the finest of all grains for feeding to ponies. They are easily digested and nutritive, and are usually fed crushed or rolled. Some ponies react unfavourably to being fed such a highly concentrated food, and may play up and become unmanageable.

Other grains often fed to ponies are barley and maize. Barley must be boiled before feeding, and is good for fattening up a pony who gets over-excited on oats. Maize is fed in dry flattened flakes which ponies adore, and is a rich energy food. Wheat should not be fed.

Bran is a by-product of the milling industry and forms an excellent bulk food for ponies. It is fed either as a bran mash (see page 113) or with other hard feed mixed into it.

Sugar beet pulp is another excellent bulk food for ponies, especially those kept stabled, *but it must never be fed dry.* About four cups of the pulp are covered with cold water and soaked overnight in a bucket. It swells up drastically and four cups of the resulting soaked pulp can be mixed with the feed. There will be enough for two or three feeds. The soaked pulp will keep for about 48 hours in a cold place. Dried pulp keeps for many months.

Sugar-beet cubes can be bought but must not be confused with ordinary pony cubes. Fed dry, they may kill your pony. If you do store both types of cubes, ensure that they are clearly labelled.

Grooming

Grooming – ensures cleanliness, improves appearance, promotes health, maintains condition and helps prevent disease.

Grooming kit:
Dandy brush – for removing heavy dirt, caked mud and dust from the coat. Should only be used very lightly on clipped ponies, or in summer when his coat is thin.
Body brush – takes out scruf and dust from the coat, mane and tail; stimulates the circulation.
Curry comb – there are two kinds: a metal and a rubber one. The metal one is used only for cleaning the body brush. The rubber curry comb is useful for removing dried mud, loose hairs and sweat, when the pony is shedding his winter coat.
Water brush – used damp on the mane, tail and feet.

Sponge – for cleaning eyes, nostrils, sheath and dock.
Hay wisp – for massage, finishing the coat and toning the muscles.
Stable rubber – for a final polish to the coat.
Hoof pick – to clean out the feet.
Mane comb – for pulling the mane and tail (see page 138).
Hoof oil and brush – for the final touches to a pony's feet.
Holder – some easily-carried container to hold all the above.

Collect the grooming kit and a bucket of water.

Put the head collar on the pony, short-track, and remove the rugs. If it is a sunny day, the pony can be tied up outside. Pick up each foot in turn and use the *hoof pick* (see page 134) to clean down from the heel towards the toe. Take care not to catch the point of the pick under the soft edge of the frog. Test each shoe, making sure it is sound and secure and that the clenches have not risen.

Never approach the pony suddenly or grasp at a foot or you may well get kicked. Start with a forefoot, standing facing the tail. Pat the

Making a hay wisp:
First, twist strands of damp hay into a tight rope about 2.5 metres (8 feet) long (not shown). Next, form two long loops at one end of the rope, and weave the rope around the two loops. Finally, pass the end of the rope through the ends of both loops and tuck the last few inches inside the final twist.

pony on the neck and then the shoulder and run your hand down the back of the leg to the fetlock, grasp this firmly and say, 'Foot'. If the pony is reluctant to lift his foot, lean on him to push his weight over on to the opposite leg. When wishing to lift the hind foot, still face the tail, pat the pony from the shoulder along the flank and down the hind leg, talking soothingly, then on reaching the fetlock, repeat the command and lift the foot firmly. If the skep is placed near each foot as it is cleaned out, the debris can fall straight into it and this saves sweeping it up afterwards.

The *dandy brush* is used next; start at the poll on the nearside of the pony to remove any mud or sweat marks with a gentle to-and-fro motion. This brush is very stiff and must be used sympathetically. Work right along the neck, the shoulder and down the nearside foreleg, then along the side, the stomach, the hips and down the nearside hindleg. Pass to the offside and put the mane over while you brush the neck, and then repeat the brushing all along the offside. (*Note:* It is usually considered that the mane should fall on the offside of the neck.) Avoid using the dandy brush on the pony's tender spots if this makes him rather restless and bad-tempered.

The *body brush* comes into action next. The object of using this brush is to reach right through the hairs to the skin, in order to clean the coat and stimulate circulation. The brush is used in short, firm and semi-circular strokes in the direction of the hair growth. After four or five strokes of the brush on the pony's coat, the brush should be drawn smartly across the teeth of the metal curry comb which is held in the other hand. Then the dust is cleaned out of the curry comb by tapping it smartly on the floor.

It is simple to build up a really good technique with the body brush. It is easier to hold it in the hand nearest the pony – the left hand while you do the nearside and the right hand while you do the offside. Stand away from the pony and working with a bent elbow and supple wrist, lean the weight of the body behind each stroke. Follow the same pattern as that described for the dandy brush, not forgetting the awkward bits round the elbows and inside the hind legs. If the pony is ticklish round his hind legs, use the brush firmly but sympathetically, holding the tail down on the hock with your spare hand. This should discourage any inclination to kick.

When you have groomed the whole body and legs, undo the head collar and fasten it loosely round the pony's neck while you brush his head, being very careful not to knock the wooden back of the brush on his bones.

Finally, the mane and tail can be brushed out with the body brush. Combs should not be used as they break the hair. To brush out a tail, stand at the side of the pony facing his quarters, and grasp the tail firmly in one hand. Hold the tail well out and brush through a few strands of hair at a time until the whole tail is neat and tangle-free.

If grooming in the stable be sure to keep dust and loose hairs from falling in the manger.

A hay wisp can be used to massage the coat and to stimulate the blood

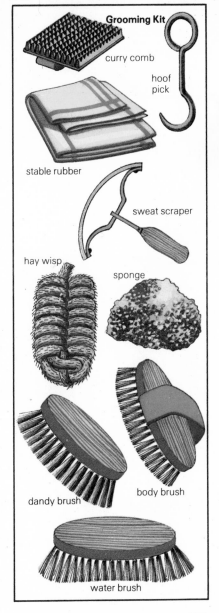

Grooming Kit

curry comb

hoof pick

stable rubber

sweat scraper

hay wisp

sponge

dandy brush

body brush

water brush

supply to the skin. It is very good for toning-up ponies just coming into work after a rest period. The wisp is very slightly dampened and banged firmly on the pony in the direction of the hair growth. It is only used on the neck, shoulders and quarters.

Wring out the *sponge* in the bucket of clean water and wipe the eyes. Wash the sponge out again then clean the nostrils. Finally, rinse the sponge again before lifting the tail and cleaning the entire dock area. The sheath should also be cleaned periodically. It is a good idea to have two different coloured sponges if you can, one kept for the head region and one for the tail area.

The *water brush* has just the tips of its bristles dipped into the water, then it is shaken before being used to lay the mane into place, leaving the hair barely damp, but in the correct position. This brush is then used to wash the feet if the weather is warm. Never wash them in cold or icy conditions. While the feet are drying, take the *stable rubber* and

Grooming

1 Clean the feet thoroughly with the hoof pick, from the heel towards the toe.

2 Remove mud or sweat marks with the dandy brush.

3 The body brush — use short, firm strokes, cleaning often with curry comb.

4 The tail is brushed with the body brush. Combs break the hair.

polish the pony's coat. The rubber is used in a flat folded bundle, very slightly dampened, and stroked in the direction of the coat's growth.

When the feet are dry, a thin coat of hoof oil is applied all over the wall of the hoof and the heels as far as the coronet.

5 Wipe the eyes gently with a clean, moist sponge.

6 Wash the sponge and then clean the nostrils.

7 Brush the mane with a moistened water brush.

8 Use the water brush to clean the feet, too. Never do this in cold conditions.

9 Polish the coat with the slightly dampened stable rubber.

10 Apply hoof oil to the walls of the feet.

Clipping

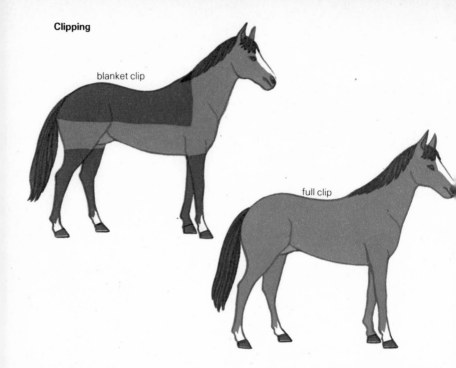

blanket clip

full clip

Grooming the pony thoroughly is known as 'strapping' and takes about 30–40 minutes once you become experienced. It is usually carried out after exercise when the skin has loosened up, the pores are open and the scurf is raised to the surface. If the pony is fed immediately after working, it should be given time to digest its meal before being strapped.

A modified form of grooming is carried out first thing in the morning and is known as 'quartering'.

Quartering:
1 Pick out the feet.
2 Sponge eyes, nostrils and dock.

3 Unbuckle rugs and turn back to quarters, brush the front of the pony and down the forelegs. Replace rugs.
4 Turn back the rear end of the rugs, and brush the pony's quarters and down the hindlegs. Remove any stains on the flanks with a sponge or water brush. Replace rugs.
Note – Roller or surcingle is left in place during quartering.

'Setting fair' is carried out in the evening. The pony is brushed over lightly and the day rug is changed for a night rug. At this time the loose box is tidied up and 'set fair', so that the animal has a comfortable night.

trace high clip

hunter clip

Clipping

Stabled ponies are very often clipped right out in autumn. This should be carried out by an expert and is usually done with an electric clipping machine. Professional clippers offer their services through advertisements in riding magazines and local newspapers. Riding schools and clubs sometimes offer such services for a reasonable fee.

Full clip – The entire coat is removed.

Hunter clip – All hair is removed except on the legs and a shaped saddle patch.

Blanket clip – The head, neck and stomach hair is removed only.

Trace clip – The hair along the underside of the neck and belly is removed. Usually for ponies at grass, turned out in a New Zealand rug.

Ponies often strongly resent being clipped, especially around the head and under the body. The hairs inside the ears must not be clipped away, neither must the long hairs on the muzzle. The clippers should not be used on the fetlocks or tendons – scissors only are used to trim these areas. The clippers must also be used with care at the roots of the mane and tail. If hair is clipped here, the new growth will spoil the pony's appearance for months.

Trimming:

The mane and tail are trimmed by a process known as pulling. This is best carried out after exercise when the skin is warm and the pores are open. Pulling effectively thins and shortens the mane and encourages it to lie flat. It is best to pull a little each day, rather than attempt the whole job at one time. Start from the withers and select the longest hairs from the underside of the mane. Twist them around your fingers and pull them out firmly and sharply. Never take top hairs from the mane and never use scissors. To prevent sore fingers, the mane comb can be used.

Back-comb the mane in tiny sections, and twist the long remaining ends around the comb before pulling them out. Take care not to upset the pony by overdoing the pulling sessions. Eventually the mane will be reduced until it is short, level and tidy, ready for plaiting if desired.

To pull the tail it must be brushed out well, then hairs from the underside are removed in a similar way to that described for the mane. The process of pulling a tail should be spread over several days so the pony does not become sore. After each pulling session, a tail bandage is put on to keep the pony's tail in shape. (See page 146.)

Washing the mane:

Equipment

Bucket of warm water,
special conditioning shampoo,
sponge,
water brush,
towel,
mane comb.

Method

1 Wet the mane thoroughly using the sponge and warm water.
2 Work in the shampoo rubbing strands of the mane between the palms of the hands.
3 Rinse thoroughly with sponge and warm water.
4 Squeeze out surplus water by hand.
5 Rub dry in strands with rough towel.
6 Brush into place with water brush.
7 Comb through carefully with mane comb.
8 Leave to dry naturally.

Washing the mane and tail

For showing or special occasions it may be necessary to wash the pony's mane and tail. It is a comparatively simple task and certainly improves the appearance considerably. Most ponies object to having water around their heads so an assistant should be on hand to hold and calm him.

Washing the tail:

Equipment
2 buckets of warm water,
special conditioning shampoo,
2 body brushes (1 freshly washed),
sponge,
towel,
tail bandage.

Method
1   Have the pony held and calmed and brush the tail right through with a body brush ensuring that all the hairs are separated.
2   Take a bucket of warm water and carefully immerse the pony's tail in it, right up to the dock, wetting it thoroughly.
3   Apply shampoo and massage it into the hairs with the fingers and palms of both hands.
4   Using the first bucket again, immerse the tail for the first rinse. Swish the tail in the water to remove as much shampoo as possible.
5   Take the second bucket and sponge clean warm water down the tail until shampoo has all gone.
6   Squeeze out as much water as possible, then swing the tail in a circular motion to dry it.
7   Take a rough towel, dry the dock area and then dry carefully down the tail in the direction of growth.
8   Brush through carefully with the clean body brush.
9   Apply a dry tail bandage and brush out the ends of the tail.
10   Leave to dry naturally.

Rinsing shampoo from the pony's mane.

Rinsing the tail, using a wet sponge.

Plaiting the mane

Plaiting neatens the mane and helps to show off the pony's neck. It is also done occasionally to encourage the mane to fall on the offside of the neck. This is considered to be the correct side and is the way the hair falls naturally in most ponies.

The mane is plaited for hunting and showing, except in classes for native ponies, and some others, when the mane is left conventionally free and flowing.

It is usual to make seven plaits along the pony's neck, nine if the mane is extra thick and five if it is rather sparse. The object is to have an uneven number of very neat and evenly plaited knobs, plus the one on the forelock.

Equipment

Damp water brush, elastic bands, mane comb,

a number of 20 centimetre (8 inch) pieces of thick thread of a colour to match the mane,

a thin bodkin,

scissors.

Method

1 Damp mane with water brush.

2 Divide into equal bunches with the mane comb and secure with elastic bands.

3 Take each bunch in turn. Remove the band, comb through and divide into three sections. Plait neatly and firmly. When three-quarters down the plait, take a piece of thread and place the centre around one of the three sections of hair. Then work the doubled thread in with that section until the plait is completed. Loop the doubled thread around the end of the plait and pull tight. Leave the thread ends hanging.

4 When all the plaits are completed, take the bodkin and the first plait, pass both ends of thread through the eye. Pass the bodkin up

Plaiting the Mane

1 First, pull the pony's mane evenly.

2 Dampen the pony's mane thoroughly.

3 Divide into equal bunches and secure with elastic bands.

4 Take each bunch in turn and divide into three. Plait neatly.

5 Secure each plait with double thread, using a bodkin.

6 Pass the bodkin up and under the plait. This doubles the plait under.

A well-plaited mane.

and under the plait close to the crest. This doubles the plait under. The bodkin is used to bind the thread around the top of the plait to hold it firmly in place, and to return the thread through to the underside of the plait, where the ends are trimmed off with the scissors.

Unless the pony's mane is very short, the plaits may need to be doubled up twice.

A little practice will enable you to make a really good job of plaiting your pony's mane. But always remember to give yourself plenty of time, and *never* leave the pony with the plaits in, or the mane could get rubbed off at the roots.

Note: It is possible to use elastic bands instead of thread for securing the plaits and bands are available in colours to match ponies' manes. Having finished each plait, a band is looped around the ends, the plaits doubled under, and the end of the band pulled over the finished plait. This does not look as professional as sewn plaits but is easier and quicker.

Plaiting the Tail

1 Some of the long side hairs on both sides are knotted together with thread.

2 Small sections of side hairs are plaited in with it.

3 Continue plaiting to half-way down the tailbone.

4 Finish with thread, then loop under to form a neat, stitched plait.

Plaiting the tail

A well-pulled, neat tail does not really need plaiting. If the side hairs are allowed to grow long for extra warmth, however, it may be necessary to plait the tail for special occasions. A small number of long side hairs on either side of the tail are separated with the fingers, then knotted together with thread. This knot then hangs down the centre of the tail and small sections of side hairs are then selected to plait in with it, continuing about halfway down the length of the tail bone. Finally the ends of these hairs are braided into a loose 'pigtail' before finishing off with thread and looping under and up to form a neat, stitched plait.

Rugs

The stabled pony cannot exercise freely and must be kept warm with special clothing. It is usual to have a day rug and a night rug. Day rugs are usually made of bright, woollen material bound with contrasting braid, and can have the owner's initials appliquéd in the corners. With matching bandages the pony looks very smart and comfortable. The rug is kept in place with a matching roller, padded to fit on either side of the spine, and straps around the girth.

Night rugs are more robust and made of stout hemp or jute, usually in their natural colour. Night rugs

A smart, easily washed nylon day rug.   A warm, hard-wearing night rug.

have a thick lining of woollen material for warmth and often have an attached surcingle, which can cause pressure on the spine. It is better to have a separate roller with pads to keep night rugs in place. In cold weather, a clipped pony will need a woollen blanket under its rug.

Rugging-up:

The rug is gathered up and thrown over the pony's back, well forward of its final position. The shaped front is arranged in place and the buckle fastened across the chest. Then from the back the rest of the rug is pulled into position so the hairs lie smoothly underneath and the rug is straight and even. The roller is placed behind the withers with the long end over on the offside. Check that it is not twisted and hangs straight. Reach under from the near-side and buckle up the roller firmly,

but not too tightly. Smooth the rug where it passes under the roller, pulling it forward towards the pony's elbows. Re-adjust the breast strap if necessary.

It is important to remember that the pony will move around constantly, lie down and get up again and so must have complete freedom of the shoulders. If the rug is not fitted properly, sore shoulders and withers and a tender back can result. When a blanket is used under the rug, it is put on in a similar manner taking care to have an ample amount on the neck. The blanket should extend beyond the root of the tail.

After the rug is put on, the surplus blanket at the neck end is folded over the rug to prevent it slipping.

Off-rugging:

First the rug is unbuckled and the roller is removed and folded up. The front edge of the rug is folded right back to the quarters. With the left hand at the centre front and the right hand at the centre back, take the rug right off in one sweeping movement over the tail. The rug can be hung neatly over the door of the box while the pony is groomed. When a blanket also is used, it can be folded and removed with the rug.

Bandages

Stable bandages are made of woollen material and are used for several purposes. The stabled pony wears them on all four legs for warmth and comfort in cold weather, and to stop the legs from becoming puffed-up and swollen when it is not being worked. On return from hunting or hacking in very bad weather, the stable bandage is put on over straw padding to dry the legs. For extra warmth in very cold weather cotton wool is often used under the bandage.

It is quite an art to apply a stable bandage correctly, for it must be put on firmly but never too tightly. Before using any bandage it must be correctly rolled, and you should acquire the habit of rolling all bandages in the proper manner each time they are removed.

Rolling a bandage:

At one end the bandage is folded and stitched across with a flat tape. Hold the bandage up with the sewn side facing you. Fold the tapes into a neat bundle and place against the sewn section. Roll the bandage

Applying a Protective Leg Bandage

1 Start just below the knee, and pass bandage around leg at a slight angle.

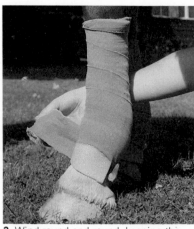

2 Wind round and round, keeping the layers evenly spaced.

firmly over and over towards yourself so that the tapes are inside, and roll right to the end.

To apply a stable bandage:
Start just below the knee or hock, and pass the bandage around the leg at a slight angle, leaving about 8 centimetres (3 inches) free at the end. The bandage should just grip firmly. Wind round and round, keeping the layers evenly spaced, right down and round the fetlock. One turn around the pastern and the angle of the bandage is naturally altered, so that it is easy to go back up the leg in the opposite direction, though still passing the bandage around the leg in a clockwise movement.

At the top, the loose edge must be turned down, and the final turn of the bandage covers this neatly. Having rolled the bandage correctly, the tapes will now be on the side. They are spread out flat and passed right around the bandage in opposite directions, then tied in a neat bow, the spare ends being tucked away under the nearest fold of bandage. The bow can be tied on the outside or on the inside of the leg but never on the front or back where it may cause pressure on a bone or tendon.

Removing a bandage:
Untie the tapes and unwind quickly by passing the free parts of the bandage from hand to hand and gathering up the slack. Never try to roll the bandage as you remove it. Hang it up to air and rub the tendons and fetlocks to stimulate circulation.

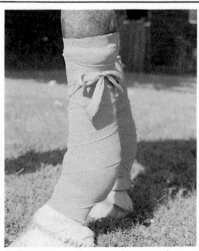

3 At the top, turn down loose edge and cover with final turn of the bandage.

4 Tie the tapes in a neat bow, on the outside or inside of the leg.

Putting on a tail bandage:

The tail bandage is made of stockinget – about 6–7 centimetres (2.5 inches) wide. It is used to save the tail from being rubbed and to improve its appearance by encouraging the hairs to lie correctly. The tail bandage should not be left on at night but is applied after grooming and exercise only.

First the tail should be lightly damped with the water brush. Lift the tail and place the first 20 centimetres (8 inches) of bandage underneath, holding the end in the left hand, and the rolled bandage in the right. The first turn is hard to make but you will improve with practice. If it seems too low, the second turn can be made above it. After the

Bandaging a Tail

1 The freshly washed tail is thoroughly brushed through.

2 The tail bandage is applied beginning at the dock.

3 It is wound evenly to the end of the tail bone.

4 Finally, it is wound back up to the dock and tied neatly.

second turn, the spare end is turned down neatly and covered with the third turn of the bandage. Continue downwards, passing the bandage around the tail until you reach the end of the tail bone, when the tapes are tied firmly but not too tightly.

Removing a tail bandage:
Do not unwind. Grasp the bandage firmly near the dock and slide down and off the tail in one fluid movement. Untie the tapes, shake the bandage loose and hang it up to air before rolling it up neatly with the tapes inside.

Head collars

A head collar is used for tying up the pony before grooming, rugging-up and so on. It should not be left on permanently as it may mark the pony's face. Head collars can be of leather or nylon, but they must be adjustable for a perfect fit, and kept clean and supple. A proper rope with a spring clip is attached to the ring at the back of the noseband, for leading or tying the pony.

For safety's sake, a pony should always be tied up with a quick release knot (see the illustration below). You should practise making this knot until it is second nature to you. To undo the knot, you merely pull the loose end of the rope. Such a knot is necessary in case your pony gets caught up or panics, and being able to release the animal with one quick jerk may avoid an accident.

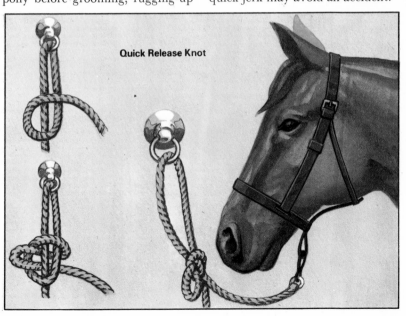

Quick Release Knot

First Aid

The most important thing to remember concerning your pony's health is to call a veterinary surgeon as soon as you suspect any severe injury or disease. Fortunately, healthy ponies living out seldom become ill. They might sustain minor injuries however, so it is a wise precaution to keep a simple kit available for dealing with emergencies. A large tin, box, or a small cupboard can be used to store the kit, but everything must be kept clean, dry and dust free.

First aid kit

Pair of 10cm (4in) blunt nosed surgical scissors.
5cm (2in), 7.5cm (3in) and 10cm (4in) bandages,
several rolls cotton wool,
some packets of lint,
bottle of colic mixture from veterinary surgeon,
saline solution in a spray bottle,
veterinary embrocation,
tin of kaolin paste,
puffer pack of antibiotic powder,
Epsom salts,
bottle of glycerine.

The pulse can be taken at the angle of the lower jaw, where an artery passes close to the bone and may easily be compressed with the finger.

The average pulse rate is 40 to 45 beats per minute for ponies. The younger the animal, the quicker the pulse rate.

The temperature is normally between 99° and 101° in ponies, and varies a little according to the age, type and feeding of the individual animal. It is taken by inserting a clinical thermometer gently into the pony's rectum for three minutes. Some ponies accept this, others object strongly, so experienced assistance is required.

Giving medicine is simple if it is in powder or liquid form and devoid of strong taste or smell, for it can be mixed in with a small, appetising meal. It is important to ensure that the pony takes the full, correct dose. A little brown sugar sprinkled over the feed should prove irresistible to the pony.

Giving liquid medicine which cannot be mixed with food is called *drenching*. This takes expertise. The pony's head is raised and the liquid is poured from a specially prepared drenching bottle down the pony's throat. When drenching, the pony's head must be lowered immediately if he starts to cough.

Electuary is the name given to the thick paste made by mixing unpleasant or unacceptable medicines with black treacle. A smooth blunt stick is used to smear the electuary on the pony's tongue, or around the back teeth.

	Healthy pony	**Sick pony**
Head	Raised	Lowered
Eyes	Clear and bright	Dull and listless
Ears	Pricked, alert	Drooping or back
Breathing	Normal (12–13 breaths a minute at rest)	Irregular, heavy, flanks may heave
Coat	Close-lying, glossy	Staring and dull
Skin	Loose and flexible	Tight and hard
Appetite	Normal	May refuse all food
General appearance	Takes an alert interest in surroundings	Looks dejected, probably resting a leg

Treatment of wounds

First aid is more commonly called for in the pony for the treatment of wounds than for any other reason. There are four types of wound. The most common is the *torn wound* in which a piece of flesh or skin receives a jagged tear from a projecting nail or barbed wire. A *bruised wound* is also fairly common, being caused by a blow or kick, a fall or over-reaching, where the hind toe strikes the back of the foreleg in action. Ill-fitting tack can cause such wounds which are then known as galls. *Punctured wounds*, especially if they occur near a joint, are serious. They are caused by stakes, nails or penetrating thorns. The entrance to the wound may be small, but the penetration very deep, and infection quickly sets in. *Clean-cut wounds* are fairly rare as they are caused by broken glass or other sharp edged material.

First, the wound must be examined and assessed. The bleeding must be arrested. Bright red blood spurting from a wound indicates a severed artery. A coin or pebble can be wrapped in a handkerchief and tied firmly above the wound to stop the bleeding as an emergency measure. Arterial bleeding requires veterinary treatment. Second, a wound must be carefully cleaned, preferably with a sterile saline solution. A deep wound should have the surrounding hair clipped away with surgical scissors. If any swelling is apparent, cold water from a hose-pipe can be trickled slowly over it for about twenty minutes.

The third stage is to treat and dress the wound. A small wound can be dried with cotton wool and liberally dusted with antibiotic powder from a puffer pack. Extensive wounds can be packed with a paste made from Epsom salts and glycerine on the smooth side of a strip of lint.

Protection to the wounded area may be possible on the lower limbs, and it is necesary to hold the dressing in place over extensive wounds. Cotton wool is wrapped around the wound over lint, and the area is then bandaged, lightly to allow for possible swelling.

Small wounds should heal rapidly, but the more serious ones need constant care for some time. Unless the pony is immunised against tetanus, it should be given an injection by the veterinary surgeon, who will also examine the wound and advise on any special care.

Common wounds

Girth galls are caused by an ill-fitting girth, and often by the soft condition of the pony. The soft skin behind the elbow is affected. The pony should not be ridden until the condition has improved, and the gall has been treated. It the skin is intact, it may be hardened and healed by applications of methylated spirit or salt water. Broken skin may need cortisone ointment to hasten the healing process. A new type of girth should be used, preferably a leather Balding girth, or one of the string variety. Rubber tubing can be used to encase the girth, or a wool pad

Hosepiping with cold water relieves swelling and heat in the legs, thus reducing pain.

can be used under the girth in the affected area.

Saddle galls range from a minor rub to a severe swollen abrasion. They are caused by badly-fitting saddles, and the pony must not be ridden until the wound is virtually healed, when a soft numnah can be placed under the saddle. A hole is cut in the numnah to accommodate the wound.

Kaolin paste dressings are applied to saddle galls, and when the skin heals it is gradually hardened off with methylated spirit or salt water. The saddle must be changed or re-stuffed to prevent a recurrence of the injury.

Broken knees result from a fall, usually on the road or hard ground when the surface of one or both knees is injured. The area might be only lightly bruised, or the fall might be severe enough to expose the knee bones through the broken skin. Except in the very mildest of cases the verterinary surgeon must be consulted. Broken knees are hose-piped gently for long periods three or four times daily to minimise the swelling. In severe cases, poultices of kaolin paste are applied and held in place by a leather kneecap lined with lint. The pony's knee should never be bandaged.

Cracked heels occur when the pony's legs have been exposed to wet conditions or not dried properly after being washed. The pony may go very lame. The veterinary surgeon will supply a special lotion which

If allowed to stand for long periods in mud, a pony may develop cracked heels.

must be bandaged on, and the heels must be cared for constantly until completely healed.

Lameness

There are many causes of lameness in horses and ponies and it is important to determine first which leg is affected, then to try to discover the cause of the disability.

To find which leg is affected, the pony must be trotted out slowly in hand. If the lameness is in a fore-leg, the pony will nod its head every time the sound leg touches the ground. Lameness in a hind leg can be detected by watching the pony from behind as he is trotted away from you. There will be a pronounced rise and fall of the highest part of the quarters, and the affected leg is that on which the corresponding hip is raised.

Having found the affected leg, it must be examined carefully, to find areas of pain, heat or swelling. Most lameness occurs in the foot of the pony, so this should be checked first, comparing it constantly with the opposite, sound limb.

Stones may be wedged between the shoe and the frog: they may bruise the foot and the lameness may persist after removing them. *Tubbing* is the term given to the treatment of foot injuries by immersing them in a saline bath. The affected foot is well washed, then placed in a bucket of warm water, to which a handful of Epsom salts has been added and dissolved. Hot water is gradually added as necessary, testing the temperature constantly with the hand. Tubbing is carried out two or three times daily for periods of about 20 minutes, then the leg is carefully dried. It is

accepted and enjoyed by most ponies. Other conditions of the foot which can be relieved by tubbing are *pricked sole*, *corns* and *nail binding*, all caused by bad shoeing. In these cases the shoes should be removed before treatment begins.

If the foot of the lame limb is sound, the examination must proceed up the leg, but specialist diagnosis is usually required. Sprained tendons show up clearly, with swelling and considerable heat. Hose-piping and kaolin paste poultices are used to reduce the pain and professional treatment is needed.

Common ailments

Colic is a severe stomach ache caused by sudden changes in the diet,

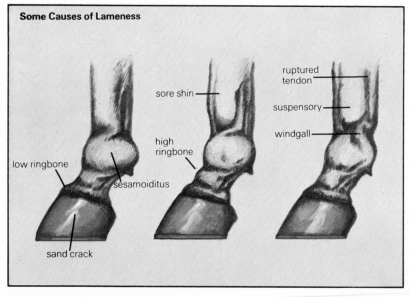

Some Causes of Lameness

sore shin

high ringbone

low ringbone

sesamoiditus

sand crack

ruptured tendon

suspensory

windgall

Poulticing the Foot

On examining the lame pony's foot a deep puncture is found in the sole (1). The hoof is cleaned and a poultice applied to the wound (2). An old sock is used to keep the poultice in place (3). Then a thick protective bandage is applied (4). A plastic bag is put over the dressing and secured, to keep the poultice clean and dry (5).

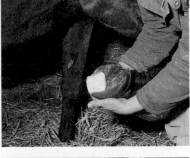

chronic indigestion, ingesting sand from sparse pastures, watering or exercise after a heavy meal, or a chill. The indications are unmistakable. The pony kicks at his belly, snaps at his flanks, straddles his legs and may throw himself on the ground and roll. The veterinary surgeon should be called without delay.

Emergency first aid measures are called for. The pony should be covered with a light rug, and walked round. If available, a special colic drink from the first aid box can be given as a drench. The pony will be in severe pain and should be kept on the move until the veterinary surgeon arrives to give the necessary injection.

Coughs and *colds* usually occur when a pony is brought off grass and stabled. All work must be stopped and it is advisable to isolate the pony from others. The stable should be warm but with plenty of fresh air. The pony should be rugged-up and bandaged. The discharge from eyes and nostrils must be wiped away constantly with cotton wool and saline solution, burning the swabs after use.

Bran mashes should be offered, although the animal may refuse all food for a few days. Hay should be put in the haynet, then a kettle of boiling water poured slowly through it to soften it. Cough mixture made into an electuary can be given and affords great relief. Mild liniment is applied to the throat if the cough is severe. If catarrh develops, the veterinary surgeon may advise steaming. To steam the pony's head, a handful of soft hay is put in the bottom of a bucket. A teaspoonful of friar's balsam or eucalyptus oil is added, then a cup of boiling water is poured on. The pony is encouraged to inhale the vapour for about five minutes and is usually afforded some relief.

Sweet itch is a skin condition caused by the allergic reaction of the pony to small biting insects, pollen or even sunshine. Midges are common during the summer months, and attack the pony from one hour before until one hour after sunset. If a pony suffers from this allergy, it should be brought into the stable during that period every day, and the stable itself treated with fly spray. The pony's skin can also be treated with repellent. If no action is taken, the pony will rub the itching areas of his body, usually the mane and all around the tail root and croup. The affected areas may be rubbed raw, and must be treated with a veterinary preparation to soothe and heal them.

Ringworm is a fungus infection caught from other infected ponies, perhaps by using an infected grooming kit. Circles of bare skin show on the pony where the hair has come away. Stop grooming him, and treat the areas with a special veterinary fungicidal lotion which is painted on. The rugs should be thoroughly cleaned and disinfected, as should the grooming equipment, and the pony must be isolated until he is fully recovered. A similar disease is also found in ponies where there are small round areas of bare skin. It is called *pustular dermatitis* and, unlike ringworm, is generally found only in the girth and saddle region. It is an infectious disease, spread by stable dust, saddlery and grooming equipment and must be treated methodically with the prescribed ointment until cleared up.

Bots are the larvae of gadflies,

A pony being bothered by swarms of flies. Eggs of the bot fly can be seen on the body.

which lay their eggs on ponies' skin in the summer. The eggs are licked by the pony and swallowed. Eventually they hatch into larvae in the stomach. When present in quantities in the pony's stomach, bots have a weakening effect. Whenever eggs are seen on the coat of the pony they should be removed and burned. Some preparations made for worming horses and ponies also contain ingredients to destroy any bots living in the animal's stomach.

Warbles show as lumps beneath the skin of the pony's back. The lump indicates the presence of a maggot: the larva of the warble fly. While the maggot is growing and developing it must be left alone, until it eventually makes a small hole through the pony's skin and makes its exit. It is important to leave the warble alone during its growing time, for if it is killed while still beneath the skin, an unpleasant, thickened lump is permanently formed. Warbles are often found around the saddle region, and the pony should not be saddled and ridden until the exit holes are discovered and treated with antiseptic ointment or antibiotic powder.

Riding

To produce a perfect pony and to ride him well, it is necessary to think about his structure and the way in which he moves. If you consider the mechanics of the pony you can apply the aids (see page 163) intelligently, and simple schooling will make any pony a better ride.

The pony's skeleton is strongest in the front, just below the withers, where the ribs are deepest and form a large, strong framework. As the ribs extend towards the loins they get smaller and the back is weaker. Large muscles run along the top of the ribs. This immensely strong section is where the rider should sit and have most of the body-weight centred.

The huge muscles of the hindquarters provide all the pony's impulsion or power. The rear end of the pony can only be controlled by the leg aids of the rider. When turning, the pony uses his hindquarters first to push the body into the turn, then the forehand, or front, follows through.

To turn a pony, the leg aids must be given to get the quarters underneath the body, then light rein pressure indicates which way the forehand should go. Too many riders try to turn their ponies by merely pulling on a rein.

To understand how to get the best out of a pony, we will examine the correct ways of riding at all paces, how the pony moves and reacts, and how best to control him.

Mounting

Check that the girth is tight and that the stirrups have been pulled down. Stand on the nearside, with the left shoulder towards the pony; take the reins, properly separated, in the left hand. Place the left hand, with reins, on the withers.

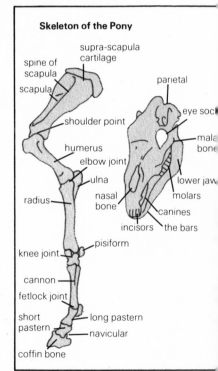

Skeleton of the Pony

supra-scapula cartilage
spine of scapula
scapula
parietal
shoulder point
eye sock
humerus
mala bone
elbow joint
ulna
lower jaw
nasal bone
molars
radius
canines
incisors
the bars
pisiform
knee joint
cannon
fetlock joint
short pastern
long pastern
navicular
coffin bone

Use the right hand to help put the left foot in the stirrup, and turn the toe downwards. Pivot to face the pony, and take the waist of the saddle in the right hand. Spring lightly off the right foot to an upright position, weight slightly over the pony's back.

Swing the right leg over the saddle, without kicking the pony's quarters, simultaneously removing the right hand to the front of the saddle. Settle gently into the centre of the saddle. Finally, place the right foot in the stirrup.

U.S. Cavalry Method

Check girth and stirrups. Stand on the nearside.

Take up reins in right hand on the withers. Stand close to the pony and take the stirrup in the left hand.

Place left foot in stirrup, pressing the knee against the saddle. Take hold of the neck or mane in the left hand.

Jump off the right foot and pause, weight in the left stirrup.

Swing the right leg over the saddle. Settle gently into the centre of the saddle.

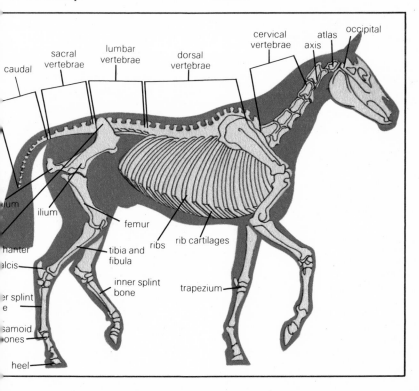

caudal

sacral vertebrae

lumbar vertebrae

dorsal vertebrae

cervical vertebrae

atlas
axis

occipital

...um

ilium

...hanter

...lcis-

...er splint
...e

...samoid
...ones

heel

femur

tibia and
fibula

ribs

rib cartilages

inner splint
bone

trapezium

Mounting

1 Take down the stirrup irons.

2 Hold pony with reins in left hand.

3 The left foot is placed in the stirrup.

4 Spring, pause, with weight over pony.

5 Put right foot in iron; check left iron.

6 Take reins and prepare to ride off.

Dismounting

1 Take feet out of stirrup irons.

2 Swing right leg over pony's back.

3 Bring legs together, slip to ground.

4 Hold reins to prevent pony moving.

Finally, place the right foot in the stirrup.

Advocates of the Orthodox Method of mounting maintain that facing the tail initially ensures that mounting will be easy if the pony should move. Unless performed in an agile manner, however, the saddle could be pulled against the pony's spine and displaced. In the Cavalry Method, the saddle is not held at all and the pony is controlled with the reins held in the normal riding position at all times during the mounting procedure.

Dismounting

It is usual to dismount on the near-side of the pony.

Remove both feet from the stirrups. Lean forward with left hand and reins on the pony's neck.

With the right hand on the pommel of the saddle, vault off, keeping the right leg clear of the pony's back. Land on the toes, avoiding the pony's forelegs.

Take the reins near the bit to hold the pony.

Cavalry Method

Take the reins in the right hand on the pony's neck. Grasp the neck or mane in the left hand.

Free the right foot from the stirrup and, leaning forward, swing the right leg over the pony's back. Pause, then place the right leg on the ground.

Use the left hand to free the left foot from the stirrup.

Take the reins near the bit and hold the pony.

The Orthodox Method of dismounting has the advantage of speed and safety over the Cavalry Method, and is safer if there is a possibility of the pony moving forward.

Both mounting and dismounting should be practised until they can be performed fluidly without unbalancing the pony. They should be practised from the offside as well as from the correct nearside, in case of emergency.

The seat

In riding, everything depends on having a good seat, for a good seat ensures good balance, and with good balance comes good hands. With good hands the rider is assured of control and security, and thus gains confidence.

A good seat is a combination of balance, suppleness and grip. A good rider is balanced and poised at all times, with such a position that he can apply grip instantly when necessary before balance is lost.

The rider sits *in* the saddle rather than *on* it, with the seat well down in the central lowest part, balanced on the seat bones. To find the natural, correct position, let the legs hang down naturally with the thigh and knee just held against the saddle flap with the minimum of muscle pressure. The feet, free of the stirrups, should hang relaxed.

If the stirrups are adjusted to the correct length, the iron should hang level with the instep of the foot while the leg is in this position. The feet should be placed in the stirrups so that there is no twist in the leather. This is achieved by turning the front part of the iron outwards. The ball of the foot is pressed against the tread of the stirrup iron and, when the heel is pressed down into the correct riding position, a natural grip is formed in the knee and thigh. The lower part of the leg is kept slightly back, and is free to apply aids close to the girth. The toes should point forward – turned out and the knee loses contact with the saddle, turned in and the calf loses contact. Above the saddle, the body should be gracefully erect with slightly hollowed back, shoulders back and chin naturally raised, so that the rider looks forward between the pony's ears. The arms should hang down naturally, elbows close to the body, forearms and wrists supple and relaxed.

The hands

Good hands are the hallmark of a good rider. There should be a straight line from the bit, along the reins through the hands and along

A good riding position with the rider sitting well into the central part of the saddle.

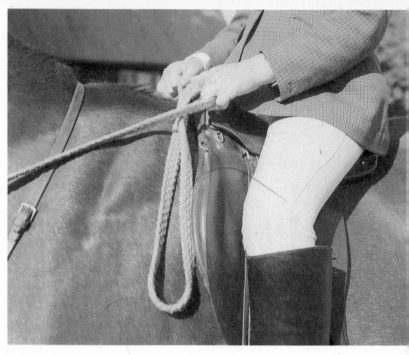

Holding the reins in both hands.

the rider's arms to the elbow. Good hands are light and flexible, being able to give and take instantaneously.

The hands are always used in conjunction with the seat and legs. They must be kept level and steady, and the action used is rather like squeezing out a sponge. The pressure of the fingers giving the squeezing movement should relay enough information to the pony's mouth. When the pony responds the hands relax again.

The reins are held in both hands. With a snaffle bridle, the rein passes between the third and little fingers

of each hand. The slack end of the rein passes between the thumb and forefinger of each hand. The hands are held level and about 10 centimetres (4 inches) apart. If preferred, the reins can be held outside the little fingers.

Occasionally it is necessary to hold both reins in one hand. With a snaffle, the left rein is taken between the third and little fingers of the left hand and across the palm, the slack passing between the forefinger and thumb. The right rein can either go between the forefinger and thumb, or between the first and second

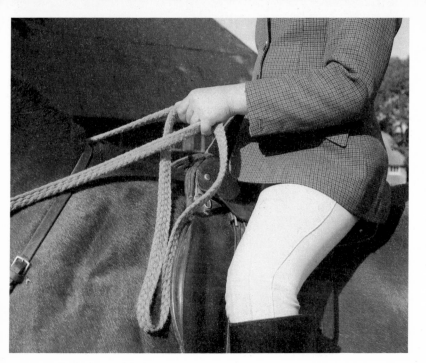

Holding the reins in one hand.

fingers of the left hand, the slack passing between the little finger and the palm.

The aids

The aids are conventional signals used to convey the rider's wishes to the pony. Young ponies are schooled or trained to obey the aids. A well-schooled pony is obedient to very slight and subtle signals; an un-schooled or disobedient pony may need very definite aids, perhaps backed up with a light tap from a schooling whip behind the girth.

The natural aids are the voice, the hands, the legs and the seat. The artificial aids are whips, spurs, martingales and other devices.

Natural aids:

The legs create impulsion in the pony. Impulsion can be thought of as energy. The legs also guide and control the pony's hindquarters. To increase impulsion, the legs are applied to the pony's sides, equally, and to control the hindquarters, the legs are used indpendently, behind the girth.

The hands on the reins control the front, or forehand, of the pony and

The Walk

regulate the impulsion created by use of the legs. The hands also guide the pony, check its speed, or allow pace to increase.

The voice assists in controlling the pony. Most ponies are schooled initially from the ground, on the lungeing rein, and learn many commands and tones of voice. Later the voice can be used in conjunction with the other aids to get the best performance from the pony.

Artificial aids:

A stick is useful in teaching a disobedient pony to respond to the aids. A cane about 65 centimetres (26 inches) long is best, and can be held in either hand. It is carried in the palm with about 15 centimetres (6 inches) protruding in front of the hand. When it is carried correctly, the end points towards the pony's opposite ear. To teach a pony to respond to leg aids, the aid is given and reinforced by a short sharp tap just behind the rider's leg. It takes considerable practice to change the

reins to one hand and to apply the stick correctly. Spurs are used only by advanced riders to give very subtle aids.

The walk

How the pony walks:

The ordinary walk is a natural movement in four-time. The legs are moved in a set sequence, one at a time. The sequence is near hind, near fore, off hind, off fore.

Aids for the walk:

Back and seat muscles pushed down and slightly forwards.

Squeeze legs gently with equal pressure. Ease the reins, letting the hands go slightly forwards.

The well-schooled pony will walk on, but the sluggish pony may need a more definite leg pressure or even a kick with both heels just behind the girth. The voice aid WA—LK can be given slowly and drawn out. If the pony still refuses to move, repeat the aids and tap a stick behind the girth.

The pony should walk on with long free stides. Only the lightest contact with reins and legs is necessary, unless the pace slackens, when a little more leg pressure must be given.

Turning at the walk:
To ride a straight line, an even feel is maintained on both reins and the calves are pressed lightly against the pony's sides. To turn left, increase the pressure of the right leg very slightly, lean from the waist slightly to the left and increase the feel on the left rein. To turn to the right, reverse the procedure.

Halting from the walk:
Indicate to the pony that a command is coming by pushing the seat down and squeezing the knees. Slightly increase the contact with the pony's mouth by tightening the fingers on the reins, and simultaneously closing the calves to the pony's sides. The pony should halt neatly, with all four feet standing square.

The trot

How the pony trots:
The trot is a pace of two-time, and the pony moves its legs in diagonal paces. The left diagonal consists of the near fore and off hind striking the ground together, the right diagonal consists of the off fore and near hind.

Aids for the trot:
While the pony is going forward freely at the walk, a light feel is maintained on the reins. To increase the pace to a steady trot, squeeze with both legs just behind the girth. As soon as the pony obeys, relax the pressure, re-applying it only if it is necessary to maintain the pace. At the slow trot, the rider can sit still in the saddle. This is known as sitting to the trot. With a short striding pony this can be very bumpy and uncomfortable, but is a good exercise and teaches balance, especially if practised without stirrups. Sitting at the trot enables the rider to feel

The Trot

each of the diagonals quite clearly and to recognise them.

Rising at the trot is really just a trick, and comes very quickly. The weight is taken on the knees, and as the bump of a diagonal stride is felt, you lift yourself slightly out of the saddle, coming down again on the next stride. You will find yourself rising and falling rhythmically with the hoofbeats of the same diagonal. After some work at this pace it is possible to ride for a while on one diagonal, then to miss a beat before rising on the other diagonal, which is beneficial to the pony.

Turning at the trot:

To turn at the trot the legs must maintain the necessary impulsion, so that the pace does not slacken or become unbalanced. To turn left, use the left leg gently on the girth, and the right leg with firmer pressure just behind the girth. The left rein is used to turn the forehand to the left and the right rein is eased

The Canter

sufficiently to allow the movement without losing contact. To turn right, the aids are reversed.

To decrease pace from the trot:
Stop rising to the trot, sit well into the saddle with a straight spine, close the calves against the pony's sides and feel the reins gently until the pace slows, either to the walk if this is what is required, or to the halt. The pony should decrease pace smoothly and in a straight line. As soon as the animal obeys, the reins

and leg pressure can be relaxed and the pony rewarded with the voice or a pat on the neck.

The canter

How the pony canters:
The canter is a pace of three-time and so three hoofbeats are heard at every stride. The pony is said to *lead* with a certain leg, and it is important to be able to distinguish with which leg he naturally leads.

The Gallop

If a pony is leading with the left leg for example, and you try to ride a sharp right-handed circle, the pony will be completely off-balance and could cross its legs or even come down in a bad fall. The leading leg also affects the rider's seat, so it can be seen that this rather sophisticated pace can only be mastered correctly after gaining experience at the slower speeds.

When the pony leads with its near fore, the off fore and the near hind touch down together and push the animal forward, then the near fore extends to the ground, followed by the off hind. An experienced rider can sit well into the saddle in a very relaxed position at the canter, which is then the most comfortable of all paces. When a pony is schooled as a youngster, it is taught its manners at the walk and trot, and when it is going really well, the canter is introduced, and the pony is trained to lead with either leg at the rider's instruction.

Aids for the canter:

It is easiest to break into a canter from performing a trot in a wide circle.

First, the reins are shortened a little, and you must stop rising and sit well into the centre of the saddle. To canter a left-handed circle, the pony must lead with the near fore in order to remain balanced. Apply pressure from both legs, the left leg firmly against the girth and the right leg well behind the girth to prevent the hindquarters swinging out. The left rein is felt slightly more than the right, and the pony should break into a smooth canter. The rider should naturally sway from the waist with the rhythm of this pace keeping the shoulders back and the head up.

When cantering on the near fore, the rider's left shoulder will naturally be a little in advance of the right as he leans slightly towards the centre of the circle. The pony must be taught to go into a controlled canter

from a slow trot for it is very uncomfortable for the trot to get faster and faster before the cadence changes.

The canter should be practised equally in left-handed and right-handed circles, so that both rider and pony can perform with either leg leading. The canter should always be controlled, for at this fairly fast and free pace the pony might decide to play tricks, to pretend to see monsters in the hedgerows and shy away, or to lower his head to put in an unseating buck.

To decrease pace from the canter:

Close the knees firmly against the saddle; sit up straight, with the seat down and forward and gently draw in the reins until the pony slows to the desired pace or to a standstill if required. When the change of pace is achieved the legs and hands are relaxed and the pony is rewarded with either some praise or a pat on the neck.

The gallop

How the pony gallops:

The gallop is the fastest pace, and is very exhilarating for both pony and rider. It is not merely a fast canter, but a distinct movement in four-time: near fore, off fore, near hind, off hind.

Aids for the gallop:

A pony must only be allowed to travel at speed when it is safe to do so. In the gallop the ground is covered very quickly, and so there must be plenty of room in which to manoeuvre and to stop. To get the pony going, the reins should be shortened, the hands lowered, and the seat and legs are used to drive the animal on. As soon as the pony is galloping, the rider takes the weight on to the knees and pivots forward, hands low on the pony's neck, head kept up to look between the pony's ears at the scenery rushing past.

Turns at the gallop must always

be made gradually, by inclining the body towards the direction of the turn.

To decrease pace from the gallop:

Some ponies get very excited when allowed to gallop, especially in company with others, and can be difficult to stop. They put their heads down and keep on going. The first thing then is to raise the pony's head, sit up in the saddle, close the legs against the girth and draw in the reins gently. The voice can also be used to steady and stop the pony, and he should be praised when he decreases pace.

Improving your riding

As a good seat is the essence of being a good rider, it is useful to carry out exercises to improve it, and to help acquire a natural balance. A series of exercises can be performed while sitting in the saddle on a well-mannered pony. They help you to relax and to become supple and more graceful. At first the exercises are carried out while the pony is standing still, but later, some may be carried out at the walk, and even at the trot.

Pivoting is done from the waist, first to the right then to the left and repeated several times. The reins are taken in the left hand, then the body and head are slowly turned around to the right as far as possible. You look back over the pony's tail and place the right hand on his quarters.

Pause and mentally check that both legs have remained in the correct position, knees gently gripping, heels down. Turn slowly back again, change the reins to the right hand and repeat the exercise to the left.

Touching toes helps to train you to keep the legs in the correct position regardless of the movements of the upper body. It also helps to supple the back and shoulders. Sit up holding the reins in the left hand. Take the right hand and hold it out at shoulder level to the right, extend it over and down to touch the left toes in a smooth, fluid movement. Both legs must be kept in the correct position. At first you may not be able to reach the toes but regular exercise will loosen up the spine until you can achieve the right position. Repeat, touching the right toes with the left hand.

Backbending entails sitting correctly in the saddle and gently bending backwards with a hollow back until your head touches the pony's quarters. Again, the legs must remain still. You then sit up again using your tummy muscles only, not by pulling on the reins!

Exercises without stirrups are excellent for improving the balance. The stirrups are either removed completely or crossed over the pommel. Trotting slowly in fairly small circles soon teaches a correct position in the deepest part of the saddle, but care must be taken to keep the heels down and to avoid gripping with the calves.

Exercises

The first three pictures show the rider
'going round the world' which is
performed in an even, flowing movement
rather like the scissors on a vaulting
horse in the gym. The pony is standing
very quietly without being held. Touching
toes is helpful in learning to keep the
legs correctly placed at all times.
Backbending teaches suppleness. Here
the leg has moved too far forward.
(Training shoes, while all right for
exercises, might catch in the irons if used
while riding.)

Exercises on the lunge are really excellent, because someone takes care of controlling the pony while the rider is able to give complete attention to the execution of the various exercises. The pony can be held stationary, or sent on at the walk or trot, describing a large circle, while an attendant holds the lungeing rein and whip. The rider can knot the reins so that they do not flap about, then perform all manner of movements, with or without stirrups. The arms can be raised, folded, held on the head or waist and the body can be inclined sideways, forwards or back. Whether or not stirrups are used, the legs should be kept in the correct position at all times, and when they are found to have moved, the exercise must be repeated until the position is corrected.

Bareback riding is the term for riding without a saddle. It enables the rider to obtain perfect contact with the pony's back and to stretch the legs down into their most natural position before pressing the heels firmly down, which closes the thigh muscles.

Blanket riding is as beneficial as bareback riding. Fold a small blanket into four and place it on the pony's back in the saddle position. The blanket is held in place with a

Bareback riding helps to improve the seat by teaching the rider to obtain good contact.

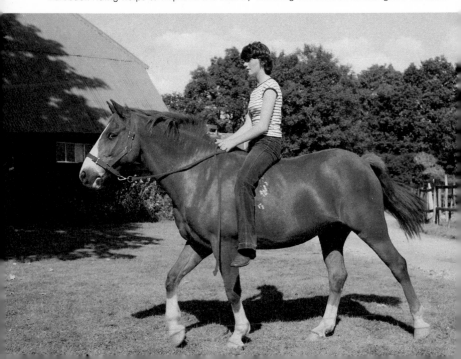

surcingle, and helps the rider to maintain a better grip on the pony's back than in bareback riding. The contact with the pony is excellent and exercises can be performed quite safely, even at the canter and over low jumps.

Second steps in riding

Having acquired a good seat and hands, and learned to ride at the natural paces, getting on and off the pony without difficulty, and stopping smoothly, some finer points of riding can be attempted. Elementary dressage movements and jumping are quite simple and enjoyable for both pony and rider.

Balance and collection:
The pony is said to be balanced when his weight, and that of his rider, are correctly distributed. The pony's head and neck form the governing factors in weight distribution, and by their position, alter the animal's centre of gravity. A pony becomes balanced through the development of the muscles of his back and hind legs during periods of special exercising, known as schooling.

The pony is schooled on undulating ground at slow, steady paces, with many smooth starts, stops, turns and circles. Once a pony is going in a truly balanced manner, it can be taught collection.

Collection is the term given to concentrated energy in the pony, when the hocks are very active and the body is collected into a shortened form. The jaw is relaxed on a light rein, and the pony has maximum control over his body and legs and can instantly obey the lightly given aids of the rider.

True collection comes from getting a great deal of impulsion in the hindquarters of the pony by using the legs on the girth, then carefully controlling this with the reins. For dressage work, a double bridle is used and the two bits aid collection. The bridoon or snaffle raises the pony's head to the correct position, then the use of the curb rein encourages the pony to bend his head at the poll, arch the neck and relax the jaw. With correctly applied leg aids, the pony is then ready to execute all manner of movements.

Dressage is a French word meaning the training of a riding or carriage horse, and a pony schooled in elementary dressage will give an enjoyable and agreeable ride. Broadly speaking, the term dressage covers all aspects of training, and once the fundamental lessons of balance, impulsion and collection have been mastered, the other movements follow on naturally.

We have already discussed the natural paces of the walk, trot, canter and gallop. The first three can be modified in a well-schooled pony and form the basis of dressage tests. The walk can be extended, and the pony encouraged to stride out purposefully, or collected. In the latter, the rider uses his legs to get plenty of impulsion, with the pony's hocks well under its body. The neck is raised and arched and the jaw flexed. The pony moves forward slowly but with more elevation than in the natural walk due to greater movement of the joints, and is ready to be given alternative aids at any time.

collected walk

The *collected trot* is light and mobile, the pony seems almost to dance along. It is usual to sit down at this pace which, although slower than the ordinary trot, looks more energetic. The *extended trot* is fast but very controlled with a moment of suspension in the air, which gives it a 'floating' apperance, and the rider rises or 'posts'.

At the *collected canter* the pony is gathered up between the rider's legs and hands and all the energy seems to be charged up in the haunches. The pace is slow and elegant. At this pace the pony can be ridden in circles, figure eight patterns and wavy serpentines. The inside leg should lead when on a circular course, and in the figure eight it is necessary to change the leading leg at the middle of the figure.

At first it is usual to slow to a trot, then strike off into the canter again, with the opposite leg in the lead. With more experience and practice, the movement known as the *flying change* can be executed. There is a split second in the beat of the canter when the pony has all four feet off the ground, and the aids are reversed during that second, so that the pony must change the leading legs. It is

exhilarating to perform and very good to watch. In the extended canter the strides are lengthened and the pony is pushed on, but is not allowed to gallop.

The *rein back* should be learned fairly early on, for it is a useful movement in many situations. A pony that will reverse in a controlled manner on command can be an

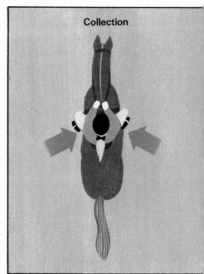
Collection

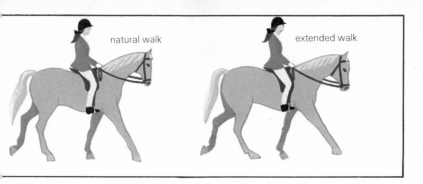

natural walk

extended walk

asset. Before beginning the movement, the pony should be standing quietly with a relaxed jaw. The rider must apply both legs and the seat to send the pony up to the bit, but instead of yielding the reins to enable him to walk on, the pressure on the mouth is retained. The pony should take even, measured steps backwards in a straight line and the rider eases the reins as soon as the desired number of steps have been completed.

If the pony shows resistance at this movement, it must be reschooled; an assistant on the ground pushes the animal's shoulders back as the rider applies the correct aids. Voice aids can be used too, and the pony should be taught to take one step at a

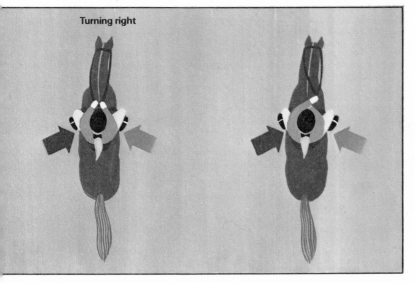

Turning right

Rein back

correct

incorrect

time, and be praised when he performs it correctly.

Two other movements which can be useful in moving a pony in a confined space, or in an emergency, are the turn on the forehand and the turn on the haunches.

The *turn on the haunches* requires the pony to pivot around one hind leg while the forelegs describe a circle around it. To execute a right turn, the rider takes both hands slightly over the right, with the right rein shorter than the left. Both legs are used firmly, the right on the girth and the left slightly behind the girth producing much impulsion, but preventing the quarters from moving out of position. The near fore crosses in front of the off fore, the hind legs mark time, moving slowly around. A full circle can be described in this way after practice,

and the turn to the left merely requires a reversal of the aids.

The *turn on the forehand* is performed when the pony is standing still and collected. To turn to the right, the hands are low, with a firm feel on the pony's mouth, the right rein slightly shorter than the left. The right leg is applied well behind the girth to push the quarters round while the left leg is used against the girth to prevent the pony moving forwards or backwards. The pony should start to pivot on the off foreleg moving his quarters round to the left by crosing off hind across the near hind. At first the pony should only be asked to take a few steps, but when both pony and rider are experienced in the movement, a full circle can be performed. At the end of the movement, the pony should be pushed straight forward

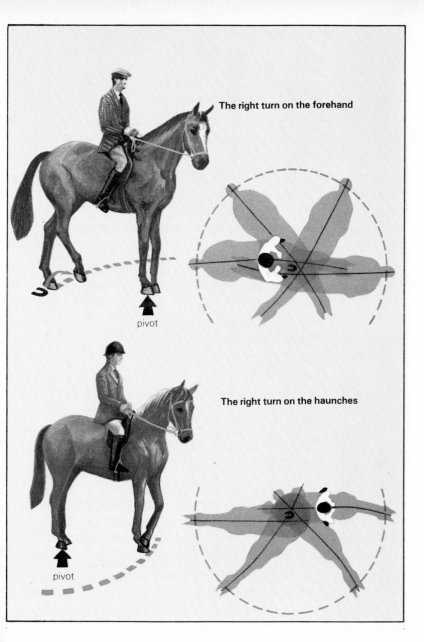

The right turn on the forehand

pivot

The right turn on the haunches

pivot

H.R.H. the Princess Anne performing a dressage test on Goodwill.

into the walk without pausing. To perform a left turn the aids are merely reversed.

Dressage tests consist of combinations of the basic movements performed in a set sequence, each movement being for a set distance or exact number of paces. To compete, both pony and rider need expert training at a riding school or club. Whether or not it is intended to perform dressage tests, it is well worth teaching the movements to all ponies, for the exercises and balancing makes them better rides and safer in unexpected situations.

Enjoying your Pony

Correct clothes make riding more comfortable, and a hard hat is an essential item of equipment. You should *never* get on a pony at any time without a protective hat or cap. The best type of hat to buy is made of fibreglass, with a separately moulded brim that snaps off in a bad fall and saves injury to the face. The riding hat should fit well and should not fall off as you bend over. It should be fitted with a safety strap or harness to hold it in place at all times.

The second most important item of riding wear is a pair of solid shoes or boots. Proper jodhpur boots designed for the job are best, but they are expensive and are quickly outgrown. Good plain shoes with a proper, medium-height heel and smooth soles are quite satisfactory.

Although casual clothes may be worn for informal riding, a hard hat is always essential.

The foot can then take its proper heel-down position in the stirrup. The foot will be prevented from slipping right through the stirrup by the heel and, if you fall off, the shoe will come clear of the stirrup iron. Wellington boots and plimsolls are dangerous, as the former could easily get stuck in the stirrup, and soft shoes without heels might easily slip right through the iron. Rubber riding boots are very good, as they are shaped for riding, with narrow feet. They are reasonable in price and do not get ruined in wet or muddy conditions. Old tights can be cut down, or stockings can be used to slip over socks when putting on rubber riding boots. This helps enormously when the time comes to remove the close-fitting boots after a day's wear.

Jodhpurs are excellent for riding. They are designed and made for the purpose, and prevent the legs from being bruised and pinched by the stirrup leathers. They cost very little more than good quality jeans, but last much longer and are smarter and more comfortable. Jeans are

Jodhpurs are comfortable for riding and prevent chafing of the legs by the leathers.

perfectly acceptable for casual riding, although the seams on the insides of the legs can be uncomfortable.

For special occasions, such as showing or hunting, a specially cut jacket is the correct thing to wear. These can often be bought second-hand through the local riding club. For casual wear, a waterproof and windproof anorak with a hood is excellent.

The only gloves suitable for riding are those made of fine string yarn. Others slip on the reins or become uncomfortable when wet. To complete the riding outfit, a plain polo-necked sweater, or shirt and tie can be worn.

Riding out

Hacking is the name given to riding out for pleasure. Casual clothes plus a hard hat and sensible shoes or boots must be worn. There are certain rules for hacking, which should be followed carefully.

Riding in the country:
Find out who owns surrounding

In the show ring certain types of dress are required for the various showing classes.

When riding across farmland, you must always keep to the headlands to prevent damage to crops.

land and ask permission to ride the perimeters of the fields. This is called riding the headlands, and in wet weather the pony must be kept to a walk to avoid cutting-up the land. Always leave gates exactly as you find them. Never ride across a field with growing crops, and ride slowly past livestock. Learn to distinguish between bulls and bullocks or cows. A bull could prove very dangerous indeed. In-lamb ewes during the early spring may be very frightened by your pony, so avoid fields of sheep at that time of the year.

Take great care when riding on pathways during wet weather. If you cut up the ground, riders might be banned from the area. Never jump any gates, hedges or ditches which you might damage.

Try to find the bridle paths in your area. They are indicated on an Ordnance Survey map. Ride along them to check that they are clear and in good condition. It they are wired off or blocked, report the fact to your local authority. Check local footpaths and try to get permission to ride along them; they usually pass through unspoiled areas of the countryside. If you pass hikers, take care not to brush them or splash them with mud. Be courteous and polite at all times. Rude or inconsiderate riders get riding banned in country districts.

Riding on the beach:
This is usually banned during the summer holiday season. If you live near the sea, check with the local authorities to see when riding is allowed on the sands. The best time to go, even out of season, is in the

early morning or late evening when there are few people about. Children rushing about or playing ball may frighten your pony and cause him to bolt. It is very important to know the times of the tides when taking ponies onto the beach. Whereas a human can clamber over rocks to safety if cut off by the tide, it is no easy matter to rescue a stranded pony.

While on the beach you must not be tempted to jump the breakwaters.

Bridle paths abound in the countryside and become overgrown if not used. Regular riding helps to keep them open.

A young pony or nervous rider can be taken out hacking on the leading rein, accompanied by an older person and a quiet, experienced horse as schoolmaster.

They were constructed to withstand the buffeting of gale force waves, and are extremely solid. The sand and shingle piled against them may be treacherously soft, and a fatal accident could result from treating such obstacles as an event course.

Ponies should only be taken swimming when there is a party of riders, just in case anyone gets into trouble.

It is best to swim a pony without his saddle and to take a good hold of the mane. Do not go out too far and never go out alone. Your pony may try to roll in the sand the moment he gets on to the beach. He will start to paw with a forefoot, then sharp leg aids should be given to keep him on the move. The salt water is good for the pony's legs, but on return

Riders should keep in single file when following narrow lanes, and drivers will slow down to overtake if given the correct hand signal and a friendly smile of thanks.

home the hooves should be washed and dried, then oil applied to stop them cracking. The tack should be sponged off with fresh water, too, to remove the salt and sand, and then oiled or soaped thoroughly.

Riding on the road:

This is not advised but is usually necessary. Some people have to do all their hacking on the road, others have to endure a certain amount of roadwork before they reach their favourite stretch of countryside. Some drivers are considerate and understand that ponies may act in an unpredictable manner at times. They drive past the pony slowly, giving it a wide berth, and accelerate away smoothly and quietly. Others may give a warning blast on the horn and drive by close and fast. Your pony should be one termed 'traffic proof' but, even so, he cannot be expected to tolerate the bad driving manners of some road users.

Always ride with the traffic, keeping well into the side of the road. If you are in a group, ride in single file with the quietest ponies at the front and rear. Ride on the verges if possible, but look out for drainage gullies which could trip the pony. Never ride faster than a walk along verges with long grass. If you see a hazard approaching and there is traffic behind you, give a clear signal for it to slow down. Always smile and thank drivers with a wave when they show consideration. Never trot around corners, the surface may be worn smooth and therefore be slippery and dangerous. Never ride on icy roads. Never ride in the dark or in fog. When crossing a busy road, wait until the traffic is clear in both directions, then cross in a straight line, very smartly.

If your pony is very frightened, it is advisable to dismount and lead him quickly into a nearby gateway or drive until he has calmed down. This should only be done if the pony is causing a hazard or if you are in real danger of coming off, otherwise the pony will remember his victory and play up again on another occasion.

A pony which habitually plays up for no real reason is said to be nappy. If he is nappy on the road it could be dangerous, so he must be taught

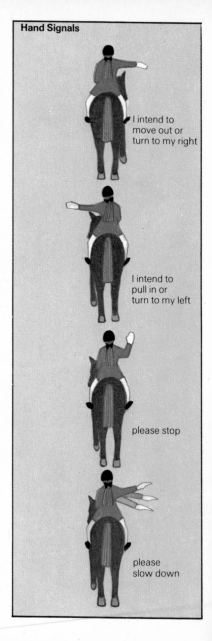

Hand Signals

I intend to move out or turn to my right

I intend to pull in or turn to my left

please stop

please slow down

manners by an experienced rider before being taken out in traffic.

Picnic rides

These are great fun in the summer holidays. It is best to go with a party of friends or other members of the local riding club. Casual clothes should be worn and the ponies should wear halters, or head collars with ropes, over their bridles so that they can be tied up during the picnic. The spare end of the rope should be looped round each pony's neck and tied securely out of the way. Food and drink are carried in rucksacks or satchels, or can be tied in packets to the metal D rings on the cantle of the saddle. You should take anoraks in case of rain or cold on the return.

Plan your route carefully, and make sure that you do not go so far that it will be dark before you return home. Ride off through the country during the morning, and keep the

Picnic rides in the country are fun and even the ponies enjoy the stop for lunch.

The Four Stages of Jumping

ponies cool. On reaching the picnic site the ponies should be relieved of their saddles and bridles and allowed to graze for a while. The saddles can be placed carefully on the ground, each with its own bridle and other belongings. They should be well away from the ponies so that they do not get trodden on and damaged. The ponies can be tied up in the shade while their riders eat the picnic lunch.

After a good rest, saddles and bridles are replaced. All the litter must be gathered up carefully to be taken home, before the party rides off on the leisurely return journey.

Learning to jump

How the pony jumps:
The pony jumps in four stages: *The approach*, when the pony lowers his head, stretches his neck and adjusts his stride.

The take-off occurs as the pony brings the hocks well under the body, raises the head and neck and springs upwards and forwards, lifting the forehead.

The period of suspension is when the pony is above the obstacle, head and neck stretched out and down, the forelegs reaching forward and the hind legs tucked under the belly.

The landing is achieved as the hind legs follow the forelegs to the ground and the head and neck come up to the normal position once more.

The rider's position:
The rider must adopt a position during jumping to interfere as little as possible with the balance of the pony. At the same time, control must be maintained, and the seat must be secure to prevent a fall if the pony stumbles, bucks with excitement, or refuses.

It is usual to have shorter stirrup leathers for jumping, which help the rider to pivot forward on the knees. The feet are placed a little more firmly in the stirrup irons also, and the heels are pressed firmly down.

The best way to learn to jump is by practising on a calm pony over cavalletti. Later they may be turned so the poles are higher, or stacked to form a respectable jump.

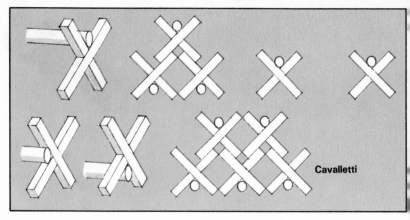

Cavalletti

During the approach, the pony's stride should be rhythmic and confident, the rider leaning forward very slightly. As the pony rises to the jump, the rider goes forward naturally, allowing the hands and arms to follow the extension of the pony's head and neck. A light contact should be retained with the pony's mouth, but the reins must never be jerked or tugged.

Only when the rider has an independent seat, that is, one independent of the reins, should jumping be attempted. In the early stages a spare stirrup leather can be buckled around the pony's neck. The novice rider can then hold on to this with one hand if necessary while negotiating a jump, so confidence is gained without hurting the pony's mouth.

On landing, the rider's weight slips back gently into the saddle and the reins are gathered in.

Cavalletti

Cavalletti are specially constructed poles which are invaluable in teaching both ponies and their riders to jump. They can be placed so that the poles are just above the ground and arranged in a series. The pony is encouraged to walk, then trot over the poles. Later the cavalletti are turned over so that the poles are a little higher, or they may be stacked (see above) to form a respectable jump.

A novice rider should learn to jump on a keen, safe pony which is unlikely to stop. A novice pony should only be jumped by an experienced rider. Lots of practice is necessary to become an expert jumper, and the pony must not be allowed to get stale so that he either refuses to jump, or jumps in a slack and careless way. Schooling should always be carried out over low jumps, and only when you intend to enter a jumping competition is it necessary to try an occasional high obstacle.

Shows and gymkhanas

Local shows are fun for experienced and novice riders alike. There are usually classes for all types of ponies at all stages of training, and for beginners as well as expert exhibitors. There are showing classes which are judged on conformation and performance, and the pony and rider must be correctly turned out and presented. There are classes for the Best Rider and classes for the pony with the Best Turnout. Family

Pony classes are for the good all-rounder. It does not have to be an exceptionally beautiful pony, just good-natured, well-schooled and in good condition. In this class, the pony may be expected to take a small jump. The Handy Pony classes vary a great deal, from an ingenious obstacle course to a straightforward test of gate-opening and turning ability. There are all manner of miscellaneous classes too, and the Fancy Dress is fun, especially when the pony allows to be dressed up.

Even novice riders can enjoy gymkana games by taking part in events on leading reins.

Jumping classes have limits on the height of the ponies entered, and correspondingly high, simple fences. Perhaps the most enjoyable jumping competition is the Chase-me-Charlie. In this the ponies line up and follow each other over two or three simple jumps. At first the jumps are very low and they are gradually raised after everyone has attempted them. A competitor is sent out if his pony refuses or knocks down a fence. The riders are instructed to keep well clear of the pony in front and to avoid accidents, and the jumps may get quite high in the final stages of the competition.

Gymkhana games are exciting to take part in and amusing for the spectators. The ponies seem to enjoy the games as much as everyone else. There are numerous events, and the ring stewards call out the rules for each one before it starts. If there are a lot of entries, the games are usually run in heats, then the winners of each ride off in a final.

The Bending Race needs practice before the event. The pony must be well-schooled and supple as well as fast. He must be able to bend at speed and stop at will. There are lines of poles set into the ground. The ponies line up, then each must gallop in and out of his row of poles, turning tightly around the last one before galloping back in the same way, to the finish. If poles are knocked out of the ground, the pony is eliminated.

Rapid turns are the order of the day as the riders compete in the exciting flag race.

In the Potato Race the rider can use only one hand on his rein and the pony must stop on command. The rider needs plenty of practice beforehand, and a straight eye, for the race entails taking a potato from a pole, or a steward, at one end of the arena, then galloping to the other end of the arena, where he must stop and throw the potato into a bucket. Potatoes sometimes bounce out again, so the pony must stand motionless while the rider leans down as far as possible to drop the potato gently. Four or six potatoes must be collected and dealt with in this way, the first one to get them all safely in the bucket is the winner. If the potato is dropped or bounces out, the exhibitor must dismount, retrieve it, mount, then try again.

In the Egg and Spoon Race the rider has to carry a wooden spoon in one hand with a potato balanced in the bowl. Sometimes hardboiled or china eggs are used instead. The rider then has to gallop down the arena and back again without losing the 'egg'. Holding the egg on the spoon with the thumb is forbidden and the winner is usually a steady, smooth-actioned pony with a calm rider.

There are many games in which music is played while the riders circle the ring. When the music stops, they rush to the centre, either to grab a pole, dismount to stand on a sack, or sit on a chair. There are fewer poles, sacks or chairs than there are competitors, and those who cannot find a base are eliminated. Eventually there is only one base left, and two or three riders race for it when the music stops for the last time.

Musical Statues is a similar game but it tests riding skill, for when the music stops the rider must halt his pony and make it stand motionless. Ponies that move, even slightly, are gradually eliminated until one winner remains.

In Apple Bobbing, the riders gallop to a line of buckets holding apples floating in water. The riders dismount and, kneeling down, try to snatch the apple in their teeth, without using their hands. When each has an apple they quickly remount and race to the finishing line.

Bobbing for apples can be rather wet, and a nudging pony isn't the best of help!

An obedient pony, a keen eye, a steady hand and a lot of luck are the requirements for winning gymkhana games. Win or lose, such events are good training for young riders.

There are lots of games in which the ponies may compete, and they must be rested between events, taking the saddle off whenever possible. After a show, the pony should be taken home as quickly as possible. It should be encouraged to stale (pass water) by shaking straw underneath its belly and whistling softly; then a drink of chilled water, that is water with some hot added to take the chill off, is put in the stable. The pony should be given a hot bran mash, and left with water and hay to rest through the night.

Travelling to shows

If you decide to enter competitions in several shows, it may be necessary to transport your pony in a horsebox or trailer. You may be fortunate enough to have a trailer, or friend with whom you can share. In any case it is important to teach the pony to load and unload without any fuss.

Teaching your pony to load may take patience. The best way is to leave a trailer in the field. The pony gets used to seeing it there and will not mind approaching it closely. After a few days, a bucket of food is shown to the pony and placed inside the trailer. The pony might well allow himself to be led into the trailer without further ado in order to reach the treat. If it is impossible to try this method, then the pony must be bandaged against possible knocks, and led in a determined fashion towards the trailer's ramp. If the pony baulks, he should be encouraged to go forward and it may help to lift a foreleg and place it firmly on the ramp to give the pony confidence. Often, a bowl of food will entice the pony aboard, but sometimes more drastic methods are necessary.

Helpers can stand either side of the pony's quarters and, looping hands behind its tail, literally 'lift' the pony up the ramp. A lungeing whip flicked at the pony's heels, in conjunction with encouraging voice aids, often works, or cold water flicked on his quarters from a yard broom can have the desired effect. Above all, the proceedings must be kept calm, and the pony rewarded when he is loaded.

Riding activities

Riding holidays are available for those who have their own ponies and can have them transported to the holiday centre. Or there are riding holidays when the ponies are provided. All

A trailer may be necessary for travelling to distant shows and the pony must be taught to load easily. Here a foreleg is being placed on the ramp to give him confidence.

types of activities are offered by the various organisations, and the holidays are suitable for children and adults of different ages and abilities. Most centres offer other sports such as swimming and tennis; some are in beautiful mountain regions, some are coastal. The holidays are advertised in all horse and pony magazines and it is advisable to send for a prospectus of the one that sounds the most interesting.

It is important to check that the activities will be within your scope and that a suitable mount will be available for you to ride. It is also important to take the advised clothing. Some riding holidays include instruction in jumping, stable management or dressage and can be invaluable. Others are mainly for enjoyment, and do not require any special riding skills, although you will probably be a better rider on your return from such a holiday.

The Pony Club has branches throughout the world.

In this latter category are the *Pony-trekking* holidays. People who have never sat on a pony before can go on these. The ponies are sturdy and very quiet, and each rider is allocated a pony which he cares for and rides throughout the entire holiday. Each day, long leisurely rides are taken through different parts of the beautiful countryside, and packed lunches are carried. There is no galloping or rushing about, the pace at all times is calm and peaceful. Rider and pony soon build up a fine working relationship and most trekkers are very reluctant to leave their new-found friend.

Joining a riding or pony club: membership of a local or national riding or pony club can be of great value to any rider, whether or not he owns a horse or pony. There are rallies at which various types of instruction are given, meetings at which other riding enthusiasts are present, and members' shows. Some clubs have instructive courses, followed by

Ponies are refreshed between rally events.

voluntary tests, and the officers and committee are always very helpful to the novice in all aspects of pony care and management.

Hunting is for the more experienced rider who has learned to ride at all the natural paces and is confident enough to jump a natural obstacle within the pony's capabilities. The pony used for hunting must be strong and safe in traffic and with hounds, and it must not be likely to tick at other horses and ponies when crowded. A pony must be very fit to undertake a day's hunting, and a pony living out in winter should only be allowed to stay out with hounds for about two hours.

The best way to be introduced to hunting is at a children's meet, usually arranged between the local hunt and the local riding or pony club. Adults can also go along to help, observe and learn. The times of the meets are advertised locally, usually in newspapers, and you must be up early to groom and prepare your pony and yourself.

Your clothes must be neat; clean jodhpurs and boots, shirt and tie, jacket and hard hat. The pony's tack must be safe and clean. If he usually has a snaffle, he might just need a martingale, or perhaps a Pelham instead for hunting. Ponies can become very excited and difficult to control in company when there are a lot of other horses galloping about. It is quite in order to hack to the meet to gain experience and to let your pony see hounds, then to

The annual carnival gives everyone the chance to dress up to join in the parade.

ride quietly home again if you wish.

There are lots of rules in hunting. The Master has absolute power on the hunting field and will send you home if you violate the major rules. These include riding into hounds, getting in front of the huntsman, whipper-in or the Master himself, all of whom can be recognised by their red coats and black caps. A pony that is coughing, or attempts to kick at hounds or other ponies will also be asked to leave. So will anyone making a lot of noise, or those who start cantering or galloping about to the annoyance of others.

When everyone has gathered at the meet, the huntsman blows his horn and, helped by the whipper-in, moves off down the road with the Master and the pack at a steady pace known as a hound jog. The rest of the field, as the followers are called, follow some distance behind and children are expected to keep to the rear. Eventually the first covert is reached and the field spreads out at a fair distance, while hounds are put in by the huntsman to see if they can find. This is a good time to check your pony's girths and to make sure that he is not sweating excessively. Hounds can be in the covert for a few minutes or an hour.

Hunting is not as it is often depicted in films or on television – with hoards of whooping people galloping about, jumping great fences, and all mixed up with hounds. It is conducted in an orderly fashion.

If hounds do find a fox, the wonderful sound known as hound music is heard. The intermittent yelps and encouraging notes of the horn give way to a deep ringing bay as the leader, then the other hounds in the pack, pick up the scent of their quarry. By this time the fox will have slipped quietly away and may have run a long way off. Hounds hunt by scent, not sight, and having picked up the trail start to run along the line, noses to the ground, still producing their unique sound. The hunt servants follow the hounds and then the field are allowed to canter after them, still keeping a fair distance.

The fox knows the countryside well and will usually take a swinging or zigzag course for some distance before hiding up again in a neighbouring wood or covert. The pack of hounds follow this scent trail assiduously. Sometimes they check, or stop, when the fox has doubled-back or rolled in manure, or paddled through a stream to destroy its scent.

Quite often the fox outsmarts hounds, and they then go to another covert to try to pick up the scent of a fresh fox.

After a strong gallop your pony may be tired. Fit, clipped hunters can stay out all day, but the thrill of the chase should not take away your thoughts of care for your pony. You

may be some way from home, and you must remember that you can only trot slowly, and walk for the last hour.

On returning home, the pony must be cool and if he isn't he must be walked about until he is. He can then be rubbed down with straw or sacking. The legs must be thoroughly checked for cuts, bruises or thorns, and treated if necessary. A bucket of tepid water can be given, followed by a hot bran mash, then the pony can be left with a haynet to rest.

At the meet: converging on the village green before a day's hunting.

The Competitive Pony

Having entered a few local shows and gymkhanas, you may find that you have the aptitude and initiative necessary to tackle more competitive events. Big competitions require a well-schooled and capable mount, lots of preparation beforehand and considerable dedication. Both pony and rider must be really fit.

Although the object of entering any competition is to try to win, it is important to be a good loser and to be prepared to learn from early mistakes.

Even experienced riders can benefit from short courses of lessons from time to time to ensure that they have not picked up any bad habits, such as faulty leg or shoulder posi-

tions or over-emphasizing particular aids. Some riding schools are excellent and teach the rider on his own pony, producing the best combination possible, and can often give good advice as to which competitions should be entered.

Showing

There are many categories in which horses and ponies may be shown – those for animals of different heights which are judged basically on conformation and performance at various paces. There are also classes for working ponies which include some low jumps. In addition there are classes for different breeds, such as

An elegant Anglo-Arab stallion on parade at the annual Ponies of Britain Stallion Show.

A magnificent Highland stallion and his stylish handler wait their turn in the ring.

Arabs or native ponies which may be shown under saddle or in hand.

The show pony is generally produced by crossing one of the native pony breeds with thoroughbred stock, and the beautiful, elegant offspring is nurtured and carefully schooled specially with the show-ring in mind.

Possibly the most popular classes at today's horse shows are those for children's riding ponies. Only ponies of quality can be successful in these classes, for they are judged on conformation and performance. The top winning ponies are usually bred from native breeds crossed with thoroughbred or Arab horses.

In riding classes at Society-affiliated shows the pony must be registered before it can be entered, and must be in possession of a height certificate. At small, friendly shows, anyone with any pony can enter to gain experience. Registered pure-bred ponies have their own classes and can be shown in hand or under saddle. They are judged against their own breed standard, and the most typical specimen, provided that it is fit and shown to perfection, will win.

To show a pony it must be trained in ringcraft. This means it must be adequately schooled for the type of class in which it will compete. It must be kept fit and well, and groomed to perfection with neatly trimmed mane and tail and constantly checked feet and shoes. It is important to know the relevant show rules for the class or event in which the pony is to be entered; to know what sort of tack is required, and how the rider should be dressed. The height of the pony and the age of the rider are also important for various classes have restrictions (see the chart on page 204).

The less glamorous but more useful cross-bred pony may be shown in the working classes where overall ability and performance carries more weight than extreme good looks.

The in-hand classes include every type of horse and pony ranging from heavy horses such as the great Shires down to the diminutive Shetland, and the animals are judged on conformation and type.

Presentation

Any horse or pony taken into the show ring needs careful presentation. Methodical grooming or strapping every day for some weeks before the show season ensures a gleaming, fine, soft coat and toned muscles.

The hair around the heels and the long muzzle hairs should be trimmed away and, on show day, all white markings must be spotless. Manes are best plaited except for those breeds which should have flowing manes, and tails may be plaited or, if already well-shaped, left free.

During transit to the show the pony's legs should be bandaged for protection and to keep them clean. A tail bandage is also applied, and a summer sheet protects the coat. The show tack must be immaculate, and carefully wrapped for protection during the journey to the show.

It is important to arrive in plenty of time in order to get established on the show ground and to get the pony settled and ready for the ring without any last-minute panics. It is best not to change into your show clothes until after the final grooming and tacking up of the pony, but obviously before the class is called to the collecting ring.

Presence

This is an elusive quality possessed by some animals, and some people. Even rather plain ponies may show well and be seen to have presence if they have been carefully schooled and enjoy their work.

Perhaps the most important aspect of schooling the show pony is to produce an impressive walk, for this is the first pace seen by the judges as the pony enters the ring. Walking in briskly and gaily with its head held well is psychologically good for the pony and a good exercise for the rider.

Careful schooling and practice before the show should have produced a good trot and a calm, steady canter with smooth transitions between the paces.

In the show ring a smart turnout is essential and refers to the presentation and grooming of both horse and rider. This pleasing combination could not fail to impress.

Ridden Classes

In the ring, the ponies circle at various paces as directed by the stewards. Keep well back from the pony in front and talk to your mount if he seems over-excited or nervous. Aim to ride well and do not cut in at the corners of the ring.

Keep an eye on the judges and stewards for orders. Eventually all the ponies will be called into line and, when your number is called,

ride in steadily and take your place next to the previous pony but not too close. Make certain that your pony stands up square and keeps alert for the judge's inspection.

The best of the ponies will be asked to give individual displays. If you are asked to do this, walk the pony forward smartly from the line and give the show in front of the judges. Give a nicely extended but controlled trot, followed by a neat figure-of-eight at the canter. If

Principal Riding Classes

Class	Height of pony	Age limit of Rider	What the Judges look for
Leading Rein	Up to 12 hands	Up to 7 years	Ridden on the lead rein. A sensible pony, compact and with smooth action and a good head carriage that looks as though it can be trusted to carry a small child comfortably and safely. Plaited mane; neat turnout; snaffle bridle; leather or smart white webbing lead rein.
First Pony	Up to 12 hands	Up to 9 years	Ridden off the lead rein. A pony with perfect manners, a schoolmaster taking care of its novice rider. Ponies walk and trot before lining up. Riders give simple individual show. Pony and rider must be well turned out. Pony judged more on safe, quiet performance than beauty.
Best Pony (12.2h)	Up to 12.2 hands	Up to 12 years	Quality pony of true pony character, totally suitable for a small child, small and compact. Asked to walk, trot and canter, must be obedient to the aids at all paces and sympathetic to the rider. Immaculate turnout of pony, rider and tack is essential.
Best Pony (13.2h)	Over 12.2 but not exceeding 13.2 hands	Up to 14 years	An exceptionally well-schooled pony of fine breeding and quality, very well-made and presented. Asked to walk, trot and canter with a change of rein, all movements controlled and balanced. Individual show can include extended trot. Pony checked for soundness.
Best Pony (14.2h)	Over 13.2 but not exceeding 14.2 hands	Up to 16 years	Pony type as opposed to a small horse or hack type. High quality of conformation and performance and the elusive air known as 'presence'. Rider must be well turned-out, competent, ensuring pony gives best performance.
Novice Pony	Up to 14.2 hands	Up to 16 years	In all other riding classes the pony must be four years of age or over, in this class it may be three years. It must not have won a first prize of £3 or more, and must be shown in a snaffle bridle. Conformation, manners and performance as well as turnout are judged.
Working Pony Nursery Stakes	Up to 13 hands	Up to 11 years	Pony is judged on performance over 2ft (61cm) jumps, not only on conformation. Turnout is important, and rider must be competent.
Working Pony (13h)	Up to 13 hands	Up to 14 years	Pony is judged on performance over jumps from 2ft 6in to 3ft (76.2cm to 91.5cm). The pony must have plenty of bone and substance.
Working Pony (14h)	Over 13 hands but not over 14 hands	Up to 16 years	Pony is judged over fences from 3ft to 3ft 6in (91.5cm to 106.7cm). The fences are of natural hunting type, penalties are given for faults and points are given for conformation, freedom of action and manners.

asked to gallop, make a smooth transition from the canter and gallop smoothly along the ring-side. Finally, rein-back and halt before the judges, standing the pony up square.

In the final analysis, the judges want to look at the ponies' conformation and ask for the finalists' mounts to be stripped. Saddles are removed and the ponies are led up to the judges for examination before being trotted out in hand. Lead your pony out and turn him away from you before trotting him briskly back in a dead straight line towards the judges. Then saddle up and remount.

If you are lucky enough to receive a rosette, thank the judge politely with a smile. Boys should take off their riding hats, girls may make a gracious bow of the head. Winners may canter a lap of honour before leaving the ring, but this must be sedate and controlled no matter how thrilled or excited the riders may be.

Sidesaddle

Perhaps the most graceful form of all competitive riding is the ladies' sidesaddle. It is essential to have a well-schooled horse or pony with a comparatively long back and a naturally low stride. This gives a more comfortable sidesaddle ride than the conventionally compact, short-backed show pony.

In riding sidesaddle, a specially made saddle, fitting the horse exactly, is used and is designed with

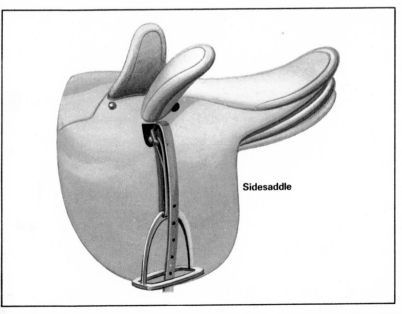

Sidesaddle

Sidesaddle, perhaps the most elegant of all the ridden classes.

two pommels. The rider sits facing squarely forward with the left leg in its natural position in the stirrup which is adjusted so that the left knee fits under the lower pommel. The right leg rests over the upper pommel, to the left of the horse's withers. The seat of the sidesaddle is often made of doeskin which gives a comfortable, non-slip seat, and a balance strap is generally fitted to prevent the saddle slipping round or out of place.

Although it seems very different, riding sidesaddle is not at all difficult. However, it is best to have a

few lessons from an expert so that bad habits do not creep into your riding. It is usual to have a leg-up to get into a sidesaddle, and once in position you must take up the correct position with the legs comfortably tucked around the two pommels. It is important to keep the right shoulder well back in order to maintain the seat and the proper balance. The hands should be held low, and you should sit up well with a good straight back, alert but relaxed. The sidesaddle gives an amazingly secure seat at all paces, especially the walk and canter. You do not rise at the trot but sit well into the saddle.

Show classes are held for side-saddle ladies' hacks in which the judges are looking for style and elegance, and a calm, well-schooled horse that goes smoothly and easily for its rider.

There are pony classes, too, some of which are designed to choose the best sidesaddle rider, while in others the pony's conformation is also taken into account.

For sidesaddle riding a special habit is worn which consists of a jacket and a matching apron-style skirt which goes over breeches and boots. It is usual to wear a bowler, shirt, tie and gloves with the habit and, for major shows, competitors in the final line-up don silk hats complete with veils, and change their ties for silk stocks.

Show Jumping

Competitive show-jumping calls for a skilled rider and a highly-trained pony. This sport has become very popular, due mainly to television coverage which has introduced it to sitting-rooms all over the world.

Most horses and ponies have natural jumping ability, and only need careful and methodical training to develop it. It is essential to receive expert help and advice before entering the larger competitions, even if you have had some success in small, local shows. The Pony Club instructors are usually very helpful and give good, un-biased advice, but it is well worth taking a carefully structured course of lessons, preferably with your own pony, before attempting a big course in the ring.

A pony and rider clearing a jump in fine style and to the obvious enjoyment of both.

For serious show-jumping it is best to invest in an experienced pony and one that has already won jumping competitions. Such a pony, if kind and well schooled, will teach you more about show-jumping than any human instructor.

A good jumping pony is short in the back with a deep girth and strong, short loins. He should have hocks said to be 'well let down', that is with plenty of length from the point of the hip to the point of the hock. He should have strong quarters and a well set on tail. It is important that the pony has well-shaped, sound feet with well developed frogs. The front is also important with a well-set neck and gradually sloped shoulders. The pony should have a very free and even trot and should enjoy his jumping, taking the obstacles calmly and accurately.

In serious show jumping the obstacles are much larger and need great concentration.

Training the Show jumper

Preliminary work is carried out over cavalletti, first at the walk, then the trot (see page 190). The sessions are kept fairly short, aiming to build up muscles and tendons as well as agility. Gradually, small jumps are added to the school and the pony is encouraged to jump these, from the trot, in random sequences and from either side. The session should be stopped before the pony gets tired or stale, and always after a good, successful effort.

Schooling sessions should be interspersed with hacking out, and small natural obstacles may be jumped during the ride. As you progress it becomes important to seek the advice of some experienced person for constructive criticism of your performance and style. When the pony jumps smoothly, accurately and well over small jumps from the trot, jumping from the canter may be introduced and some higher jumps added to the course.

Enter a small show first of all with jumps no higher than about one metre (three feet). Depending on your performance you can then go on to more ambitious shows.

Hunting helps to develop jumping ability in horses and ponies, and later on it is a good idea to enter a Hunter Trial in which you and your mount will learn to take a great variety of fences at a fairly fast pace.

When entering a Hunter Trial it is important to walk the course before the event in order to familiarize yourself with each fence and the layout of the course. Remember, you must keep the white flags to your left and the red flags to your right. There are other marker flags or arrows, usually yellow, which show the direction of the course, and also markers to indicate the start and finish. The rider must pass through these or he will be eliminated.

In the actual event you should

Pony Club Trials are very good training.

ride at a comfortable, easy pace, following the pattern you formulated in your walk around the course. You should do your best to ride accurately and well and to bring out the best in your pony, but you should not aim to win at all costs. Treat the event as an intensive training or schooling rather than a competition and you will gain valu-

Hunter Trials

borough bench

rise

wood pile

able experience. Who knows, you may also be in the ribbons, too.

In the jumping ring

For show-jumping, arrive at the show-ground in good time, check your pony then go to the secretary's tent to collect your number. Check that you have been entered in the correct classes and see if classes are running late.

hay rack

water jump

style

fallen tree

Locate the collecting ring and look at the layout of the jumps for your class. Make sure that you know the rules of the competition in which you are taking part. Just before the class you can walk round the jumps.

Having made the preliminary checks, your pony may be made ready for the ring. For show-jumping he will need a thorough warming-up session before he actually jumps in the competition, and, if you like, you can put him over the practice fence provided.

When the class is called, go to the collecting ring and wait your turn to jump. Be careful not to crowd the other competitors' mounts. There may be a considerable amount of tension transmitted to the animals which in turn could lead to some kicking or general restlessness.

When your number is called, move smartly into the ring at a brisk trot. You may canter around the edge of the ring if you wish but be sure to wait for the bell to signal before you start your jumping round or you may be eliminated.

Take the jumps smoothly and carefully just as you have practised at home, and in the correct order, and, when you have completed the course, leave the ring quietly.

Outside the ring, dismount and loosen the girths and lead your pony around to cool off. If you have done well and might be called for a jump-off, keep your pony cool and calm until the rest of the competitors have completed their rounds.

Do not be tempted to overface a young pony, or yourself, at your first few shows, but use the outings to gain experience. Aim to jump accurately rather than going all out for speed. It is most important to take the jumps cleanly and to encourage the pony when he jumps well, and to scold him quietly when he is careless.

If he does prove to be an accomplished jumper, you will learn how to push on to jump faster rounds as you become more experienced in competitions.

Eventing

This has become a very popular sport and is the best all-round test of the horse and rider's training. In eventing the horse must be calm and collected enough to perform a simple dressage test, skilled and agile enough to undertake the show-

The trailer may be used as a stable between events to feed and rest the pony.

At large two- or three-day shows it is better to hire a stable for the pony's comfort.

jumping phase and courageous and fit enough for the arduous cross-country section. The rider must also be tough, fit and strong-willed.

The rules for eventing are designed to prevent very young or inexperienced riders on small, unsuitable mounts from undertaking too strenuous a trial. Riding Clubs stage one-day events, the Pony Club stages special events for riders under 18; in America the age limit is 20.

The British Horse Society has Novice Trials which consist of three main tests: dressage, show-jumping and cross-country. The preliminary dressage test is designed to exhibit the standard of the horse's general training. The show-jumping element tests the horse over eight or 10 various fences up to a height of 1.14 metres (3.75 feet). The cross-country test covers a distance of 2.4 to 3.2 kilometres (1.5 to 2 miles) with about 18 solid fences up to a height of 1.07 metres (3.5 feet).

To compete in the British Horse Society events, you have to register your horse and yourself as owner with the Society. Your horse must be 15 hands or more and at least five years old and, to ride in the event, you must be at least 16 years of age. In America, the United States Combined Training Association registers eventing aspirants. Riders must be 14 years or more for the Preliminary Division, and 12 years or more for the Open Training Division.

The event horse is usually chosen for its outstanding characteristics at the age of four or five and then brought along slowly until ready for the exacting tests.

The event rider must be a good all-rounder, prepared to work really hard to perfect all aspects of the riding skills required. To be really successful it is necessary for both horse and rider to be expertly trained from the beginning. Before entering a major event, it is usual to enter smaller competitions with each of the event's components. For example the horse and rider gain cross-country experience by entering Riding Club trials, they gain jumping experience at local shows, and dressage experience by entering Riding or Pony Club competitions.

Gradually attaining complete fitness and confidence, horse and rider achieve the standards necessary for an event, usually taking 10 to 12 weeks to attain the required peak. Grooming and feeding are as important as the gradually increasing exercise, and this is where the skill of an experienced trainer is so useful.

The Event

On arrival at the event you must go to the secretary's tent to declare your horse a starter, and to get a map showing the cross-country course layout so that you can walk it.

After checking and unloading your horse, he should be gently warmed up for about 40 minutes, then put back in his trailer, or a show loose box with a small net of hay. It is usual to travel on the day preceding the event unless it happens to be fairly near to home.

On the morning of the big day, make an early start, feed, groom and plait your horse, have your own breakfast and then collect your number cloth from the official tent. Check the schedule, the arena in which you are to ride and the approximate time you will be called. Ride-in your horse before the competition as you have been trained to do.

Enter the arena confidently and try to remember the test by letting the steps run, like a favourite poem, through your head. For the dressage test you must wear breeches and boots, white shirt, stock and pin, a black or navy coat and a hard hat, completing the outfit with dark gloves. Spurs may be worn.

After performing the set movements of the test, salute the judges and retire from the arena, dismount, slacken the girths and lead the horse back to his box to prepare him for the show-jumping phase. You wear the same clothing for the show-jumping, but your horse may have extra items of tack added for protection if required, such as brushing or over-reach boots.

You will have about half an hour between the phases, which should give you time to settle your horse, change tack and have another quick look at the layout of the course. Try to take the jumps in a steady and unhurried fashion, going for a slow clear round rather than taking a gamble at speed. After the round return to the box.

start

finish

Cross-country riding is very exacting, calling for great skill of both horse and rider.

For the cross-country phase you will need different equipment, the most important item of which is a specially constructed crash cap. You may wear breeches, boots and gloves plus a coloured shirt, stock and sweater. Yoy may wear spurs if you wish and carry a short whip. You will have your favourite tack for riding cross-country and protective clothing and equipment fcr the horse. It is a wise precaution to have a surcingle right round the saddle, too, in case the girths break.

Ride the course at a good steady canter, again trying to jump clear and accurately rather than at speed. After the event return to the box and check your horse thoroughly for any cuts or abrasions, let him cool down, then offer a drink of chilled water. It is very important to take great care of your horse after an event which is excessively tiring for him.

Points are scored in each phase of the event and totalled to give the final results. However, win or lose, there is a great sense of achievement in having completed the tests to your own satisfaction.

Glossary

Aids The signals given to the horse or pony. Natural aids are hands, seat, legs and voice; artificial aids are martingales, whips and spurs.

Bandages Protective strips of material used to protect the legs and tail.
Bed down To lay the bedding correctly in the stable or loose box.
Bit The mouthpiece of the bridle.
Bridle Leather straps holding the bit in place.
Bridle path Designated by the local authority for the use of riders on horseback.
Breaking The term given to the earliest stages of a ridden pony's training.

Cavalletti Wooden cross-pieces so made that a pole affixed to them can be placed at different heights by turning them over. Used in schooling.
Cavesson Padded head collar and nose band, used for schooling on the lungerein.
Chestnut Horny projection just above the knee inside the foreleg and just below the hock inside the hindleg.
Clench End of the nail holding the shoe, twisted off, turned down and hammered flat into the wall of the hoof. Raised clenches are dangerous and need attention from the farrier.
Clip (1) To remove the winter coat.
Clip (2) The part of the horseshoe which fits on the front wall of the hoof.
Colic Severe pain in the digestive organs.
Colt Young male horse or pony.
Condition General fitness and well-being; the state of muscles and skin. Unwell – 'poor condition'; just up from several weeks at grass – 'soft condition'; ready for hunting, show jumping or racing – 'hard condition'; Improving physique – 'gaining condition'; Deteriorating physique – 'losing condition'.
Conformation Shape and appearance which should conform to certain breed standards and requirements.
Cow hocks Hocks turn in and are nearer together than the feet when viewed from behind.
Crest Neck's curve between poll and withers.
Crib-biting A vice, often caused by boredom, in which the horse or pony chews any unprotected wooden parts of the stable while at the same time sucks air.

Dishing A fault of action in which the lower part of the foreleg is thrown out when moving forward.
Drenching The giving of liquid medicine by pouring it down the throat with a specially protected bottle or syringe.
Dressage The art of training the horse or pony to absolute obedience to fine aids, and the performance of specialised movements.
Droppings The horse's dung.

Electuary A medicine in the form of a paste, administered by spreading on the tongue.
Ergot Small bony lump protruding from the rear of each fetlock.

Farrier A qualified person who makes and fits horseshoes.
Field The people other than the officials, who follow the hunt on horseback.
Filly Young female horse or pony.

Flying change To change the leading legs at the canter without slowing to a trot.

Foal Newborn horse or pony.

Forelock The hair hanging over the forehead.

Frog The leathery triangular formation in the sole of the hoof which acts as shock-absorber and prevents skidding.

Gall A sore place usually caused by badly fitting tack.

Gelding Castrated male horse or pony.

Girth A strap which holds the saddle in place.

Green A term used to refer to an inexperienced pony.

Gymkhana Contests and games on horseback.

Hacking Going for a ride.

Halter Used for leading or tying up; usually made of hemp or rope.

Hand Unit of measurement used in measuring the height of a horse or pony from the highest point of the withers to the ground in a vertical line. Is equal to 10 centimetres (four inches).

Head collar Leather, nylon or plastic contraption of straps worn on the horse's head. For leading, tying up and as an aid to catching up in the field.

Hogging A term used for the removal of the mane.

Hoof pick Implement for cleaning hoof.

Hound jog A slow, even trot.

Irons Metal part of the stirrup in which the rider places his foot. Must be of the correct size, for safety.

Jibbing Refusing to go forward.

Jodhpurs Specially-cut riding trousers introduced by the Jodhpur Lancers of India in 1880. Prevents chafing of the legs by stirrup leathers.

Laminitis Fever of the pony's feet often caused by too much rich new grass and insufficient exercise.

Leathers Straps attached to the saddle which hold the irons.

Livery Stables at which horses are looked after for their owners.

Loose box A stable with half door in which the horse or pony can move freely.

Lungeing Training or exercising the horse or pony using a long rein attached to a cavesson. The trainer stands in the schooling area and works the animal in circles with the aid of a special long whip and voice aids.

Mare Adult female horse or pony.

Martingales Artificial aids in the form of straps which help to hold the pony's head in the desired position.

Mucking out Cleaning the stable and removing the soiled bedding and dung.

Near side Left side of the horse. Horses and ponies are generally led and mounted from this side.

Neck strap Loose strap around the pony's neck to give confidence to novice riders.

Numnah Saddle-shaped pad used under the saddle.

Off side Right side of the horse or pony.

Over-face To ask the pony to jump higher than its capabilities.

Over-reach When the heel of the forefoot is struck with the toe of the hindfoot, causing severe bruising or cuts. A special boot may be fitted to prevent such damage in an animal that habitually over-reaches.

Paddock Enclosed area of grazing land.

Pedigree List of forebears.

Plaiting (1) Crossing of the forelegs due to faulty conformation.

Plaiting (2) Process of putting plaits into the mane and tail to enhance the·appearance.

Pulling (1) The pony takes the bit between its teeth, pulling against the rider's hands.

Pulling (2) Removal of excess hair in the mane and tail to produce a neat effect.

Quartering Light grooming to remove dust, mud or slight marks.

Rein-back To move back a few steps, in a straight line, while riding.

Roller A special girth to hold a rug in place.

Rugging up Putting on the rugs.

Saddle horse Stand upon which saddles can be placed for cleaning or storage.

Saddle soap Specially prepared soap applied to leather with a damp sponge.

Schedule The programme prepared for a show. This will show the types of competitions, the heights of the fences, plus special local rules and conditions.

Schooling Training and educating horses and ponies.

Short-racking Tying up with a short rope while mucking out or grooming.

Skep Wicker or plastic basket for collecting droppings from the stable.

Sound Term used to describe a horse fit in wind, limb, heart and eye.

Spavin Bony enlargement caused by the knitting together of the hock bones.

Splint Small bony growth between the splint and cannon bones.

Stallion Adult male horse or pony.

Strapping Thorough grooming.

Stud An establishment at which a stallion is kept for breeding.

Sweet itch Irritable condition of the skin along the crest, withers and croup. Can cause serious loss of condition.

Tack General term for all saddlery abbreviated from 'tackle', meaning harness.

Temperature Normal resting temperature of a horse or pony is 100.5° F; 38° C.

Tendons Fibres attaching the muscles to the bones of the legs.

Thrush Foul-smelling disease of the frog caused by neglect of the feet or incorrect shoeing.

Toe Front part of the hoof.

Tree The frame around which a saddle is built.

Trimming General tidying of the hairs on the head, ears, mane, tail and heels.

Tubbing Placing the leg in hot or cold water to relieve swelling, pain or inflammation.

Twitch Illegal device applied to the nostrils of a difficult or disobedient horse or pony.

Warbles Lumps in the saddle region caused by the larvae of the warble fly.

Weaving Stable vice in which the horse sways from side to side, often lifting each forefoot in turn as the body sways to the opposite side.

Withers Bony ridge where the neck joins the back.

Worms Intestinal parasites causing loss of condition. Regular dosing is necessary for their control.

Yearling Colt or filly between its first and second birthday. Thoroughbreds have their official birthday on January 1st each year, so a thoroughbred may become a yearling when only six months old or so.

Index

Useful Addresses

British Horse Society
John Blackmore
National Equestrian Centre
Stoneleigh
Kenilworth
Warwickshire CV8 2LR

British Show Jumping Association
Lt-Cmdr W. B. Jefferies (RN, Retd)
National Equestrian Centre
Stoneleigh
Kenilworth
Warwickshire CV8 2LR

British Show Pony Society
Captain Ronnie Grellis
Smale Farm
Wisborough Green
Billingshurst
Sussex

Horse and Hound (*specialist magazine*)
King's Reach Tower
Stamford Street
London SE1 9LS

J. A. Allen & Co (*specialist shop for horse books*)
1 Lower Grosvenor Place

Buckingham Palace Road
London SW1

Ladies' Side-Saddle Association
Mrs V Francis
28 Featherbed Lane
Addington
Croydon CR0 9AE

National Pony Society
B. A. Roberts
7 Cross and Pillory Lane
Alton
Hampshire

Official Eventing Organisation in USA
USCTA
1 Winthrop Square
Boston
Massachusetts 02110
USA

Pony Club Headquarters
Miss Moir
National Equestrian Centre
Stoneleigh
Kenilworth
Warwickshire CV8 2LR